Wate
A Vital Resource

Written by:

Peter Hancock

First published
September 05 in Great Britain by

ePRINT

Educational Printing Services Limited

Albion Mill, Water Street, Great Harwood, Blackburn BB6 7QR
Telephone: (01254) 882080   Fax: (01254) 882010
E-mail: enquiries@eprint.co.uk   Website: www.eprint.co.uk

ISBN 1 904904 38 6

Contents

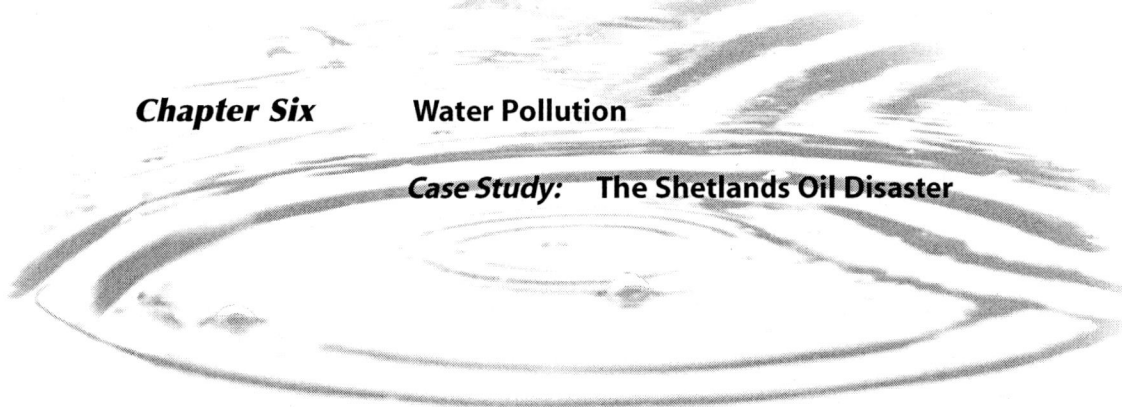

Teachers' Notes

This resource is divided into logical chapters, each dealing with a specific issue. Every chapter provides information supported by clear diagrams, case studies that illustrate each topic, as well as written and practical tasks that the students may undertake. It is designed to be used as the basis of a general study of water, or sections may be extracted and used at the teacher's discretion as part of a more general geographical project.

Pupils' tasks are divided between written work, marked ⌇ and practical activities, marked ℗ . Written work is differentiated, individual teachers being the best judge of their pupils' abilities, so that the level of work may be set accordingly. It is left to the teacher's discretion as to whether the pupils are informed of this difference, but they are coded as follows:

Simpler tasks that may be undertaken by the majority of pupils are labelled Trickle

Harder tasks, or ones that may require more enquiry, are called Splash S

More challenging work is denoted as Deluge. D

Please note:

In addition to this introduction there is a section at the back of the book providing answers to certain questions, as well as comments and suggestions referring to particular tasks.

Introduction

Earth - A Watery Planet

There is only so much water (a finite amount) on planet Earth. It has been estimated that there is 1.4 billion cubic kilometres of water, some in liquid form, some solidified as ice or held in the atmosphere as a gas. There is the same quantity today as there was a million years ago. In other words, it is a closed system and no water is added or taken away: so we drink the same water that was drunk by the dinosaurs! However, 97% of this is salt water. Of the remaining three percent fresh water, 2% is trapped in the polar ice caps, leaving a mere 1% as fresh water in lakes, rivers or trapped beneath the ground.

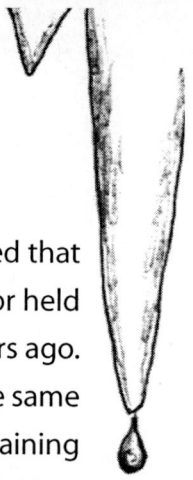

Water is constantly circulating; evaporating from the Earth's surface, rising into the atmosphere, condensing to form clouds. It returns to the ground as precipitation; sleet, snow, rain, hail, etc., runs into streams and rivers and eventually finds its way into the sea. Then the sequence starts again. It is a process known as the **Hydrological Cycle** or **Water Cycle.**
(See Figure 1, page 6)

1) Try to write a clear definition of (a) percolation (b) condensing.

For us in Britain water is something that we take for granted. Gone are the days when water had to be collected from a communal tap or well. It is always there when we turn on a tap in our kitchens and bathrooms, and we expect it to be clean. Periods of drought are infrequent, and very rarely are our supplies reduced.

However, the global picture is somewhat different. As there is only a limited and unchanging quantity of fresh water, this natural resource is under increasing demand by a growing population who need more and more water. By 2020 global water use is expected to rise by 40%. Yet even today clean drinking water is unobtainable for 1.5 billion people. There are many fundamental problems to address: more than 2.5 billion people live without basic sanitation, while water-borne diseases are responsible for 80% of illnesses and deaths.

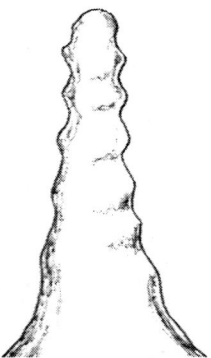

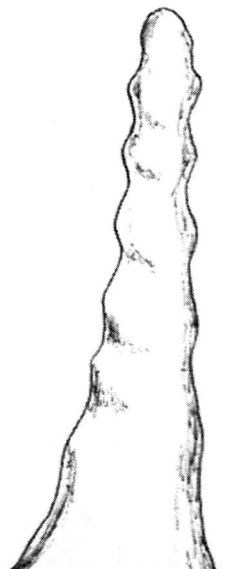

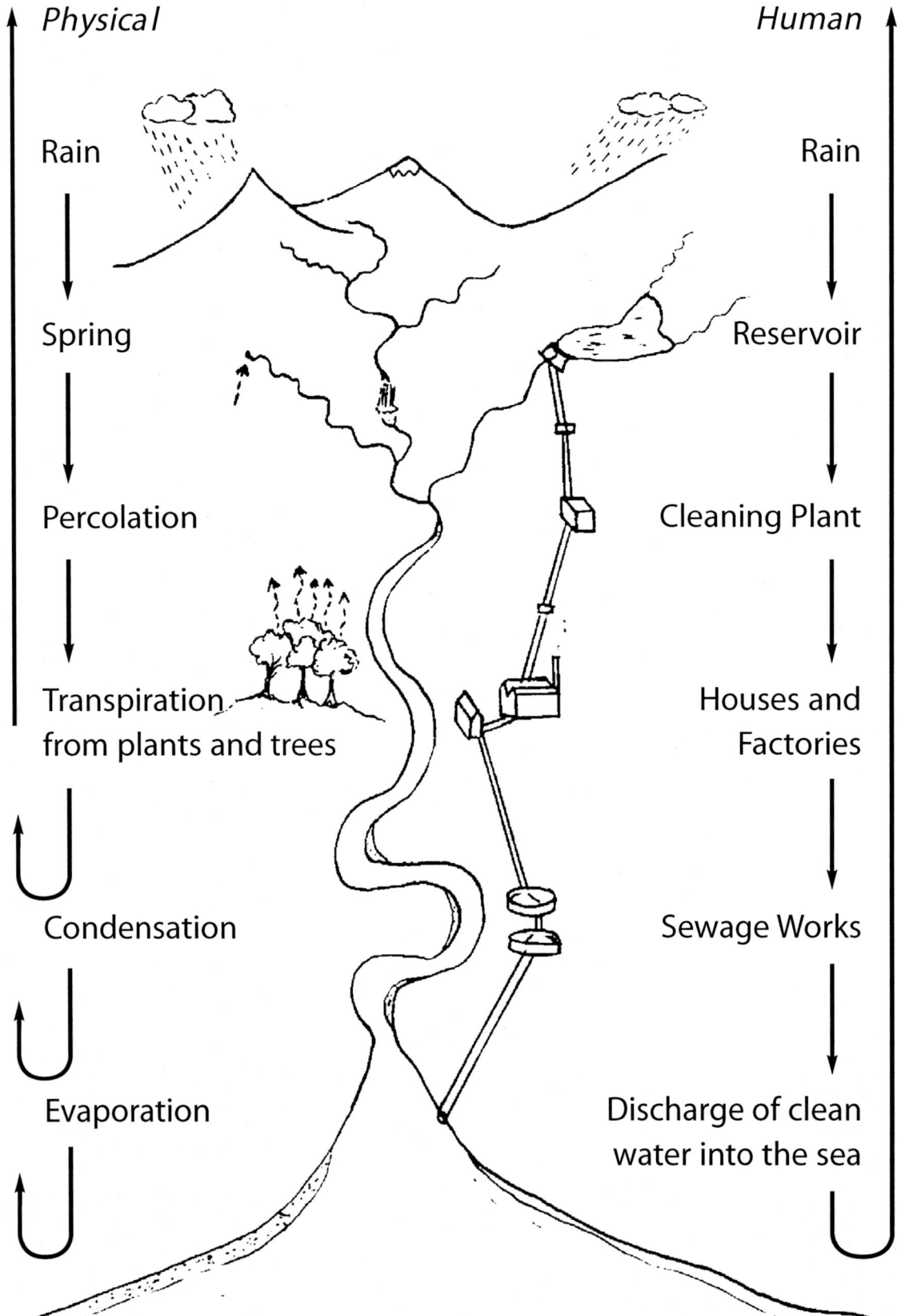

The Water Cycle
Figure 1

Physical

Rain

Spring

Percolation

Transpiration from plants and trees

Condensation

Evaporation

Human

Rain

Reservoir

Cleaning Plant

Houses and Factories

Sewage Works

Discharge of clean water into the sea

Chapter One

Natural Water Courses - Rivers

Figure 6 (page 19) shows the course of a river, from its source in the hills or mountains, to the sea.

1) **Try to think of river features that would fit into each stage, and add them to the list at the bottom. As you study this chapter add more features when you come across them.**

2) **Why do you think more erosion takes place in the youthful stage of a river, compared with the old age stage?**

The Source

Figure 2

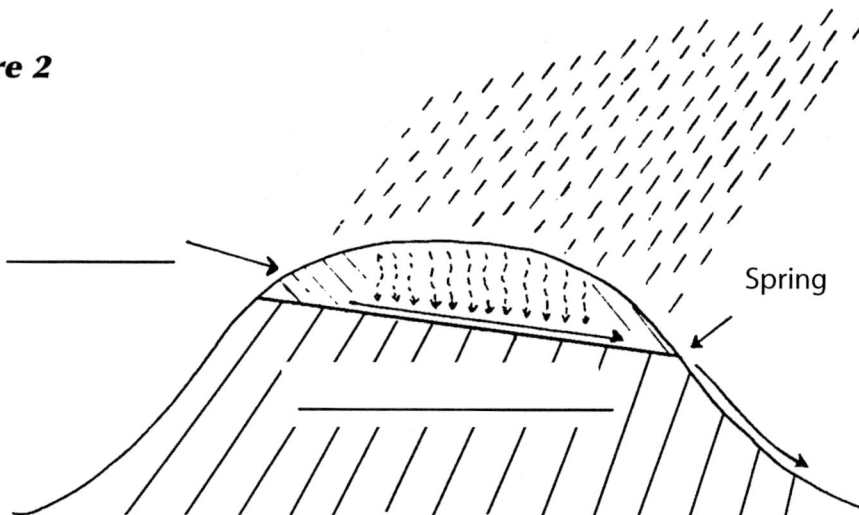

The reason why the spring is emerging from the hillside is the geology. The hill is formed from two different types of rock, one porous, the other impermeable.

3) **What is meant by geology? Use a dictionary if you are unsure.**

4) **What does (a) porous (b) impermeable mean?**

5) **Label the diagram with these words.**

Rivers often have a large number of sources. The streams later meet at a **confluence**, to create a **river system**. These can create a pattern: a common one is a **dendritic** or tree-like pattern.

Drainage Basins

Look at what happens to the rain water in Figure 3. Draw catchment areas on to Figure 4 in a similar manner.

Figure 3

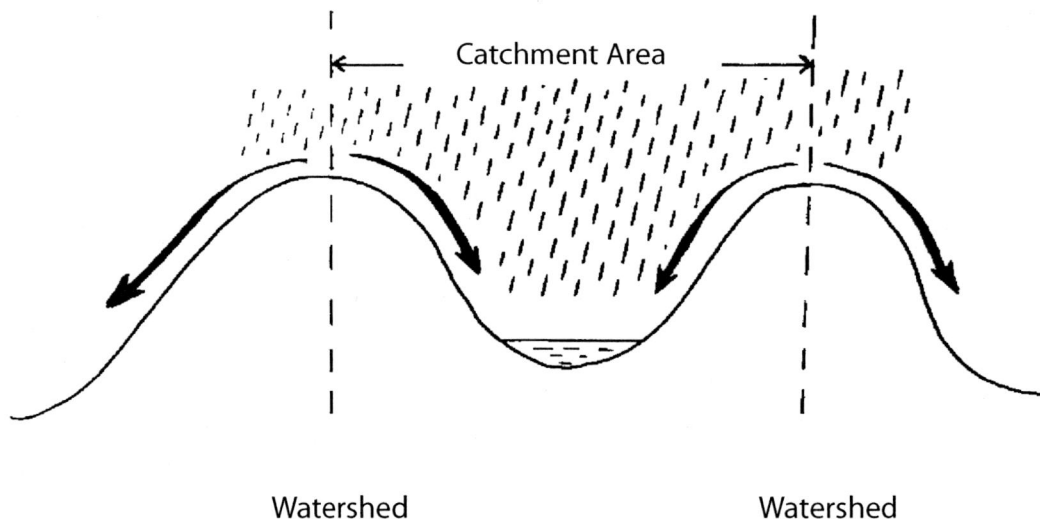

Catchment Area

Watershed   Watershed

Figure 4

Take a sheet of card and lightly screw it up. Now ease it apart and lay it on a table. Using a marble to simulate running water, identify the drainage basins. Now take a marker pen and draw on to the card the watersheds. *Note:* this random landscape more closely resembles the real world than the idealised cross sections in Figures 2 and 3.

Language

6)   **What are the other meanings of the words (a) watershed**

(b) catchment area?

Case Study: The Grand Canyon

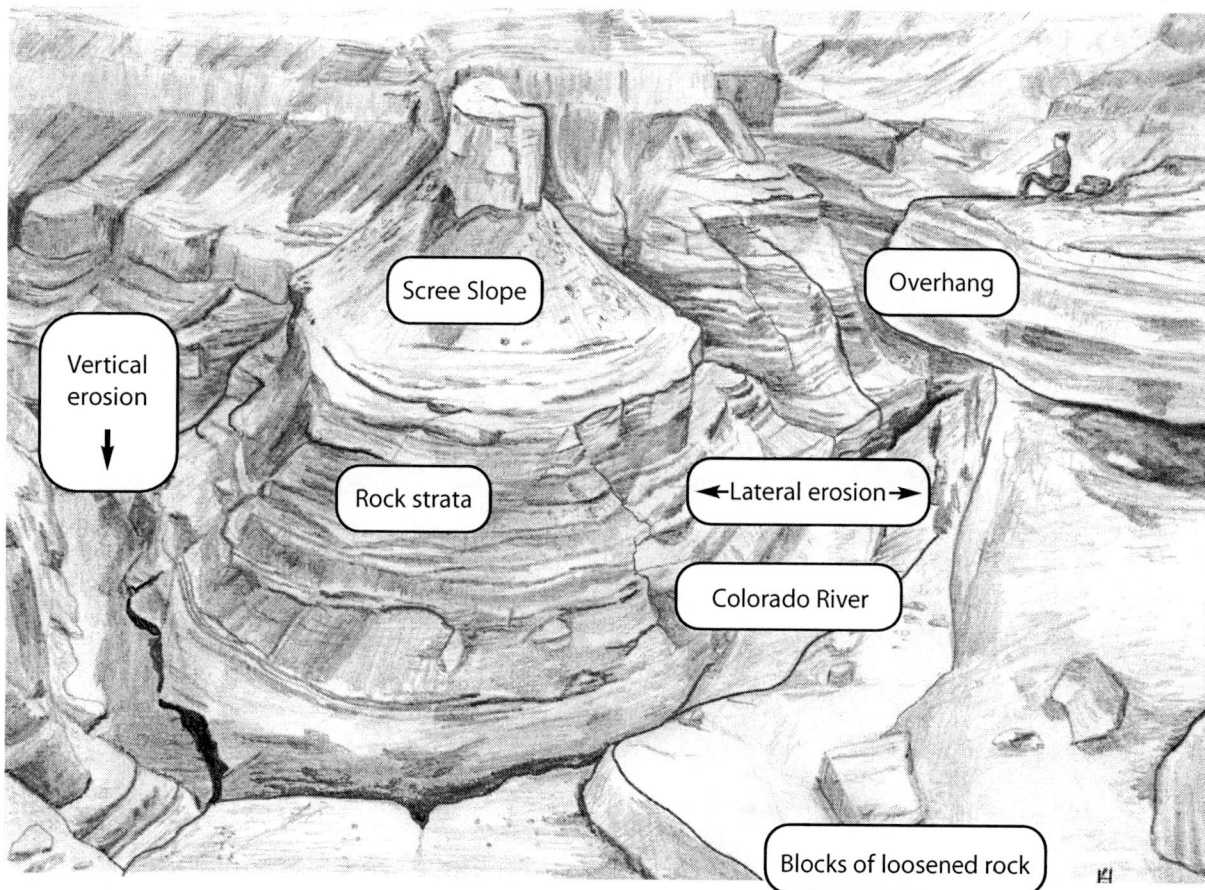

Vertical erosion

Scree Slope

Overhang

Rock strata

Lateral erosion

Colorado River

Blocks of loosened rock

Use the picture above to fill in the blanks:

The Grand Canyon in the USA has been created by the _____ River. In places it is over 1,900 metres deep and 24 km wide. It was formed as the powerful river cut rapidly downwards - a process known as _____ erosion - leaving the _____ _____ exposed. _____ or sideways erosion was far less pronounced, relying on *weathering*. Rain cut grooves in the valley sides (*physical* weathering), crystals growing in cracks crumbled the rock (*chemical* weathering), while tree roots and burrowing animals (*biological* weathering) also helped to break up the rock. This has left blocks of _____ _____ and unstable ____ _____ of loose stones, while in places harder rock that was not eroded so easily juts out forming _____.

Use an atlas to discover the names of:

(a) The state in the USA in which the Grand Canyon is found.

(b) The lake to the west of the Grand Canyon.

(c) The dam that controls the flow of water from that lake.

(d) The city which depends on the dam for water from the lake.

Try to discover more about one of the following:

(a) The story behind man's taming of the Colorado River.

(b) White-water rafting on the river.

(c) The wildlife which lives in the Grand Canyon National Park.

Try to find out about gorges that can be found in the British Isles, e.g. Cheddar Gorge or Avon Gorge.

Interlocking Spurs

These features are found in the youthful stage and are formed by the stream, trapped within its narrow, V-shaped valley, being forced to flow between areas of hard and soft rock, obstructions and boulders. They will also be seen in the mature stage, when they are more rounded and become truncated spurs.

Make a fist of your hands, and then put your knuckles together. The join between your knuckles represents the river, and the knuckles themselves, representing harder rock, are like interlocking spurs.

The Load of a River

The load of a river is the amount of silt or alluvium it is carrying. This may depend on the seasons, or the type of climate through which the river is flowing.

1) What factors will influence the load of a river?

Discharge

This is the amount of water that is carried by a river. It is measured in cubic metres per second. In other words, the volume of water that passes a certain point in one second is recorded. This may not sound much, but in a large river it may be a huge amount of water - as much as tens of thousands of cubic metres per second!

2) Is there a relationship between the load of a river and the discharge?

The Flood Plain

By the time the river reaches the old age stage, it has slowed dramatically, and now lazily meanders or twists across a broad flood plain. This, as its name suggests, is liable to flood, especially when the river is in spate. The main force of water is on the outside of river bends, while deposition occurs on the slower inside of meanders. The old truncated spurs have been eroded to leave gentle rounded banks on either side, called bluffs. To protect farms on what is often fertile land, drainage ditches may be dug, or artificial banks known as levees constructed to contain the water.

3) Using Figure 7 (page 20) mark on the following features:

(a) meanders	(d) drainage ditches
(b) bluffs	(e) the estuary
(c) levees	(f) the flood plain.

4) (a) Mark onto the river the course of the main current that will cause the greatest amount of erosion.

(b) Mark on any areas where deposition may occur.

Case Study: The Somerset Levels

Figure 5

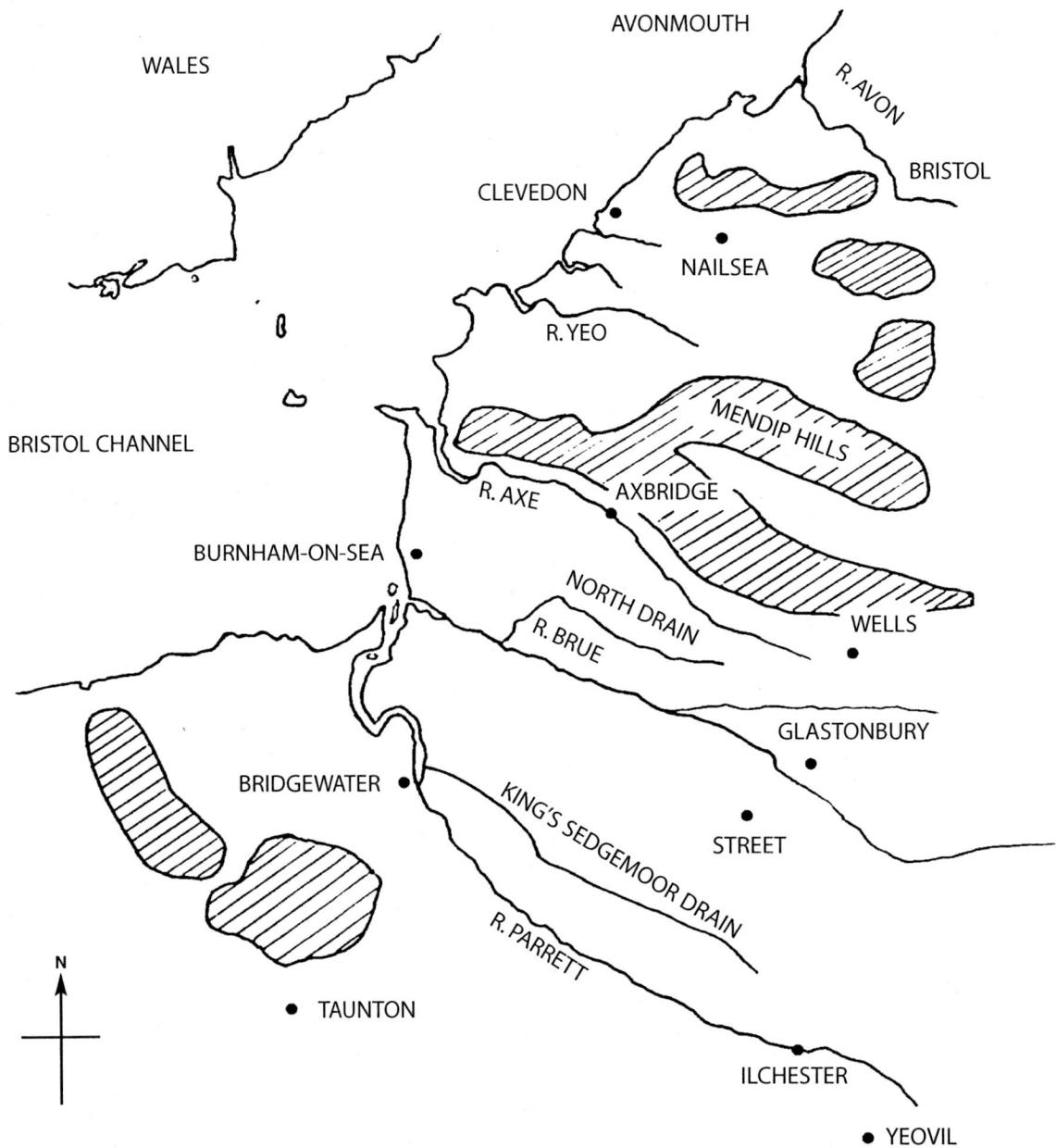

The Somerset Levels is an example of a wetland. These flood plains are low-lying and are occasionally or permanently covered with water. Other names that are linked to them are bogs, marshes, fens or peatland. Being level and low-lying these areas are at risk from flooding, either by rivers or the sea. They are a valuable habitat for a wide variety of plants, birds and small mammals.

The Area

The area of the Somerset Levels and Moors Natural Area is defined by the 10 metre contour line. It includes the flood plains of eight major rivers or drains; the Kenn, Yeo, Axe, Brue, Huntspill, King's Sedgemoor Drain, Parrett and Tone. Today it includes the largest area of lowland wet grassland and natural flood plain remaining in England. A number of ridges and knolls, such as Brent Knoll, Burrow Mump and Glastonbury Hill, rise above this flat landscape.

1) **Locate the area in an atlas.**

2) **On the map (Figure 5, page 14) colour in the low lying areas to show the land that is at risk from flooding. Then colour the high land in a different colour.**

3) **In which direction do the rivers crossing the Levels general flow?**

Its History

The area was once part of the Severn Estuary. During prehistoric times people built wooden trackways across the wetlands to reach higher ground. Gradually, over the centuries, it was drained using a system of rivers, drains and ditches (known locally as rhynes - pronounced `reens`). The man-made *rhynes* were also used to separate the wetland between commoners into small rectangular blocks.

4) **In 1685 the last battle fought on English soil took place near Sedgemoor. Try to discover the role the landscape played in the outcome of the battle.**

5) **What place name evidence can be found on the map to suggest it is an area of wetland? (Place names can often be connected with an area's history.)**

6) **Glastonbury has been connected with King Arthur and the mythical Isle of Avalon. Does the map evidence support this?**

Water Management

Today a system of ditches still carries the water away to main collecting channels. From these it is lifted into embanked rivers by pumps run by the Environment Agency. Tidal sluices are used to release the water into the sea. The level of water can be varied, so that during the summer the ditches can act as moats to keep the livestock in the fields. The Huntspill River was created in 1940 to further improve the drainage.

Wildlife

The Somerset Levels are home to large flocks of migrating birds that arrive in their thousands; wigeon, teal, shoveller and pintail duck - even starlings. The RSPB runs the 1,400 acre West Sedgemoor Reserve which sometimes has as many as 25,000 wigeon and teal over-wintering in the reed beds. During the summer months many of the duck breed in the northern regions of Europe, such as Iceland, Scandinavia and northern Russia, then migrate to the area in the autumn.

S 7) **Try to find out more about some of the birds mentioned above. You may like to plot their migratory routes on a map of Europe.**

Stewardship

Recently, conservation volunteers have helped return the Avalon Marshes to a wetland, just as it would have been 2000 years ago. This has involved cutting out certain intrusive shrubs, thereby allowing natural heathers and reed beds to flourish. (A similar scheme is being undertaken at Rainham Marshes in Essex.)

D 8) **Who do you think is responsible for looking after the Somerset Levels? Consider the factors above. Also, are there any other uses of the area that should be considered? (E.g., willow is harvested for basket-making; many tourists visit the region because of its associations with King Arthur; the M5 motorway crosses many of the rivers and drains.)**

Using a local river as an example, produce a triptych wall display to show the upper, middle and lower courses. Try to show features that may be found along the river's course. These could be divided into **human** (man-made) and **physical** (natural) features.

Try to create your own meanders.

(a) **Place a support under one end of a flat board and dribble water down the slope. How steep does the angle have to be for the water to meander?**

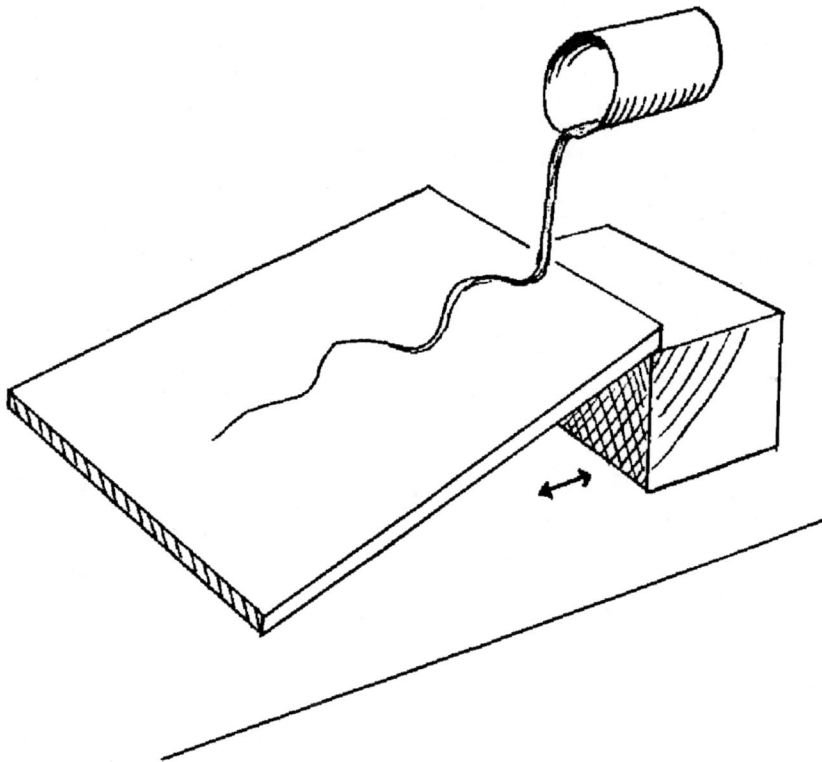

(b) **See how different materials, such as a piece of smooth plastic or rough slate, affect the flow.**

(c) **After first drying the surface, try placing plasticine obstacles in the way of the water.**

Extension Work: World River Features

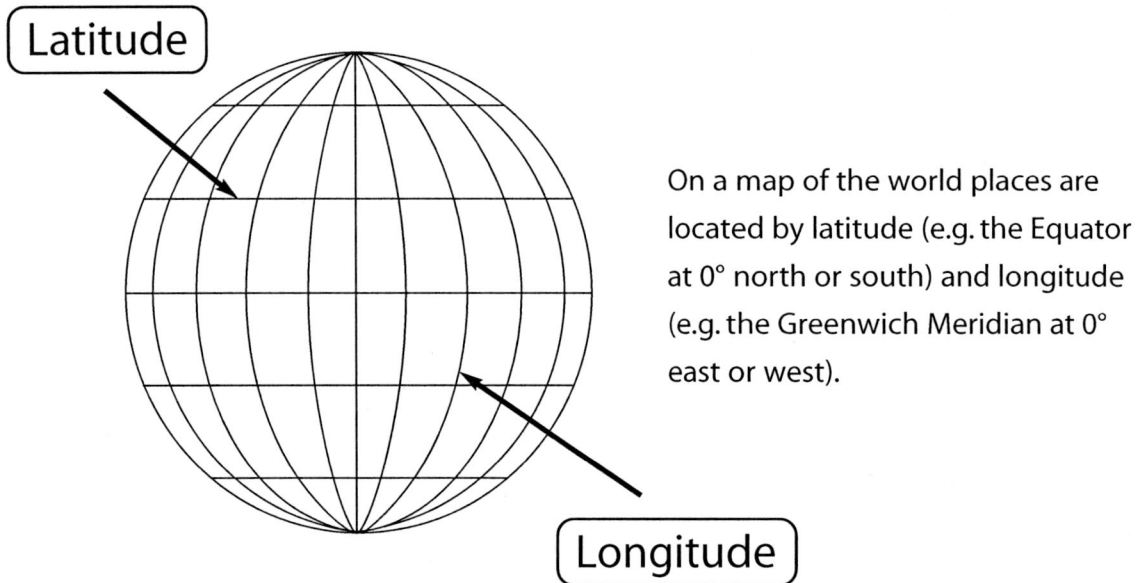

Latitude

Longitude

On a map of the world places are located by latitude (e.g. the Equator at 0° north or south) and longitude (e.g. the Greenwich Meridian at 0° east or west).

Find the following examples of river features on a world map, using their co-ordinates.

Tip: **Using an atlas, find the general location on a map of the world. Then look up the exact position on the most suitable map of that area.**

1)   Source - 1° 0` S  33° 0` E

2)   Waterfall - 5° 57` N  62° 30` W

3)   Rapids - 41° 59` N  91° 40` W

4)   Gorge - 36° 15` N  112° 30` W

5)   Confluence - 15° 31` N  32° 35` E

6)   Meanders - 49° 27` N  1° 4` E

7)   Flood Plain - 30° 27`N  91° 12` W

8)   Bluffs - 34° 13` N  92° 1` W

9)   Delta - 31° 0` N  31° 0`E

10) Estuary - 51° 29` N  1° 0` E

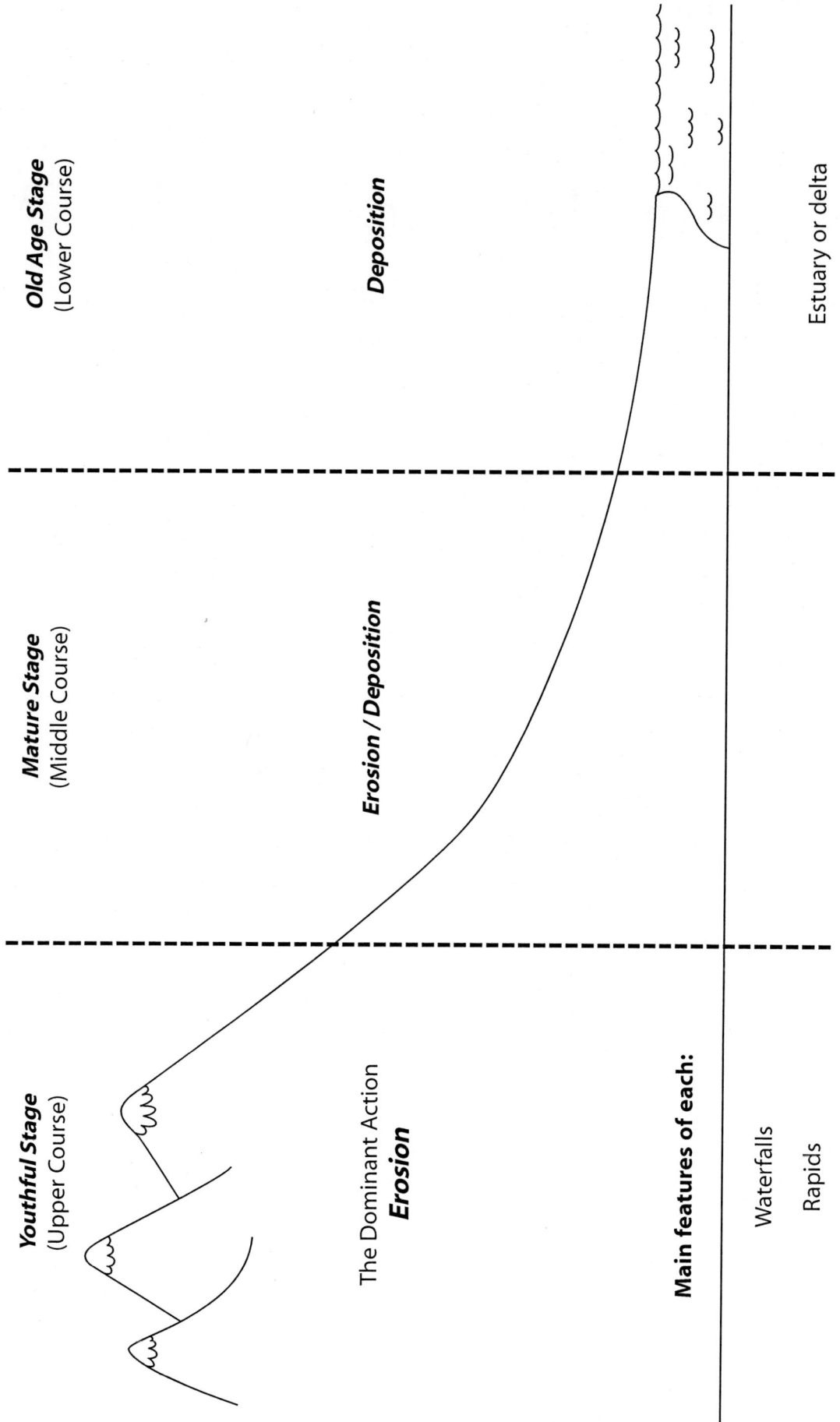

The Course of a River - Mature Stage

Figure 6

Youthful Stage (Upper Course)

Mature Stage (Middle Course)

Old Age Stage (Lower Course)

The Dominant Action **Erosion**

Erosion / Deposition

Deposition

Main features of each:

Waterfalls

Rapids

Estuary or delta

19

The Flood Plain

Figure 7

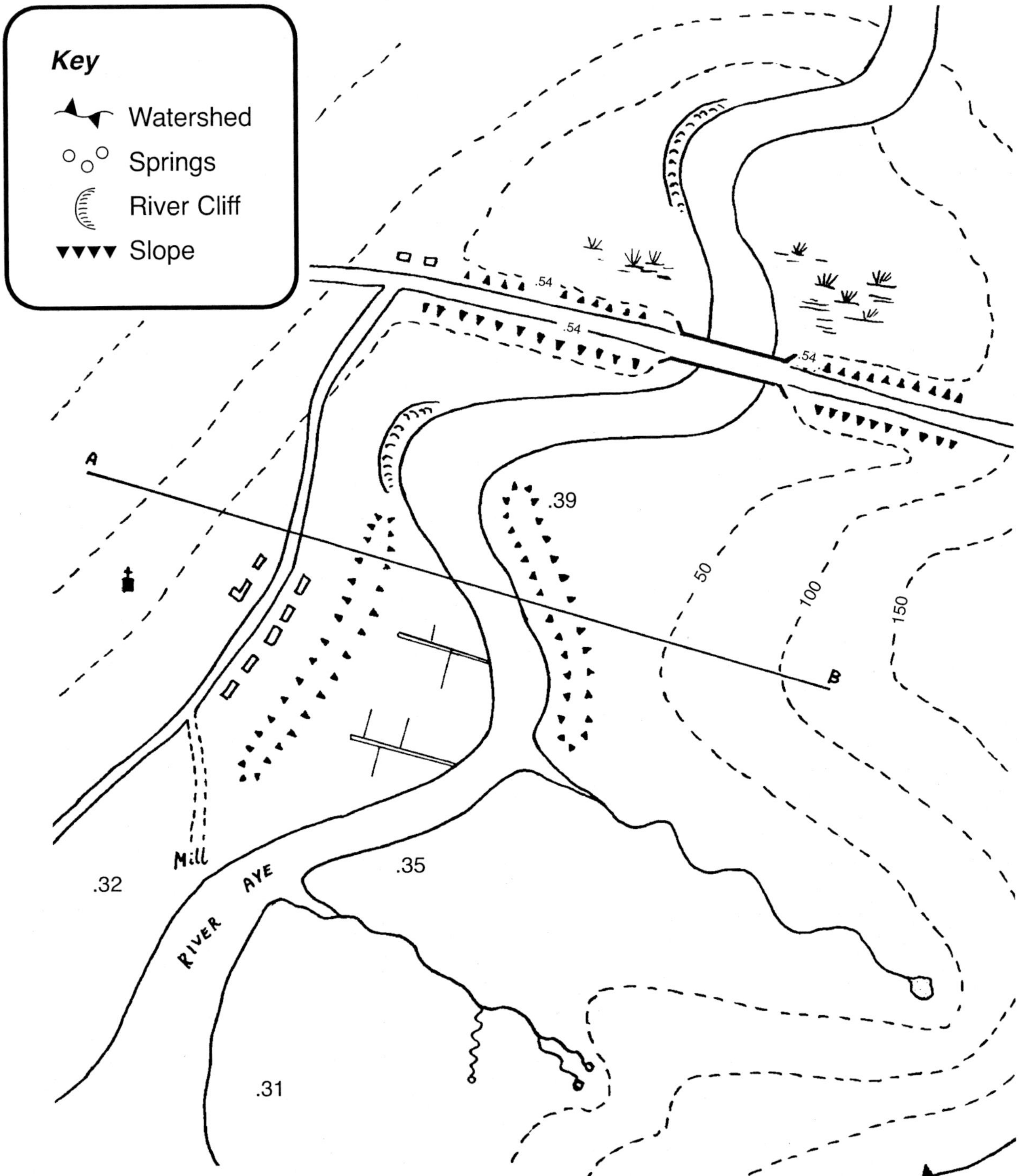

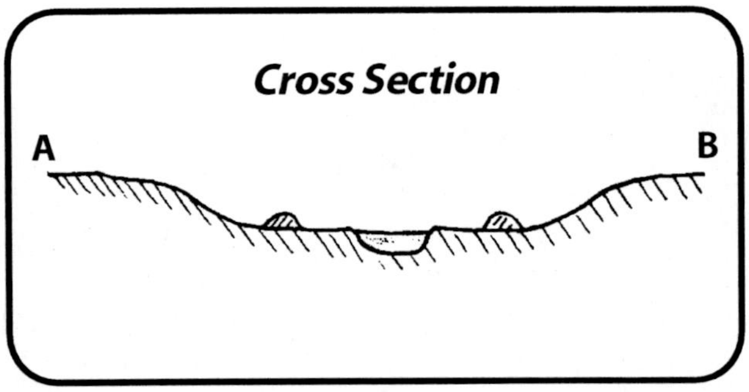

Key

- Watershed
- Springs
- River Cliff
- Slope

.54

.54

.54

.39

50

100

150

A

B

Mill

RIVER AVE

.32

.35

.31

150

Cross Section

A

B

Chapter Two

Uses of Water

It may be surprising to discover just how much water we use, often without thinking about it, for everyday tasks.

Table 1	
More Economically Developed Countries (e.g. Britain)	**Less Economically Developed Countries** (e.g. Ghana)
Washing hands under a tap - About 5 litres Flushing a toilet - 10 litres A full bath - 80 litres Taking a shower - 12 - 20 litres One washing machine load - 100 litres One dishwasher load - 30 litres A garden sprinkler for one hour - 910 litres	Water from a well - 20 litres

Saving Water

1) (a) **Can you think of any other uses of water around the house not listed above?**

    (b) **How much water do you think these tasks would require?**

2) **What could be done, both at school and at home, to reduce the amount of water that is used? Remember, your ideas must not affect people's standards of hygiene.**

3) **Why are people in less economically developed countries more likely to be careful with the amount of water they use?**

4) **Use the spreadsheet provided on page 31, or compile your own data base, in order to record how much water you use over a period of time, such as a week or month. You may like to display your results on a graph or pie chart.**

5) **Place a container in a sink beneath a tap. Allow the tap to drip slowly for an hour, then measure how much water has been collected.**

6) Calculate how much water would be lost from one leaking tap over a 24 hour period.

7) Looking at Table 1 on page 23, what could be done with that amount of water?

8) Can you work out how much water would be lost from your leaking tap in a year?

Thought: Many leaks like this go undetected for long periods from old or damaged pipes beneath the ground.

9) Look at your answers to Question 2. Choosing one or more of your ideas, design a sign that could be placed next to the place where water is being used to remind people to reduce water consumption *(the amount being used).*

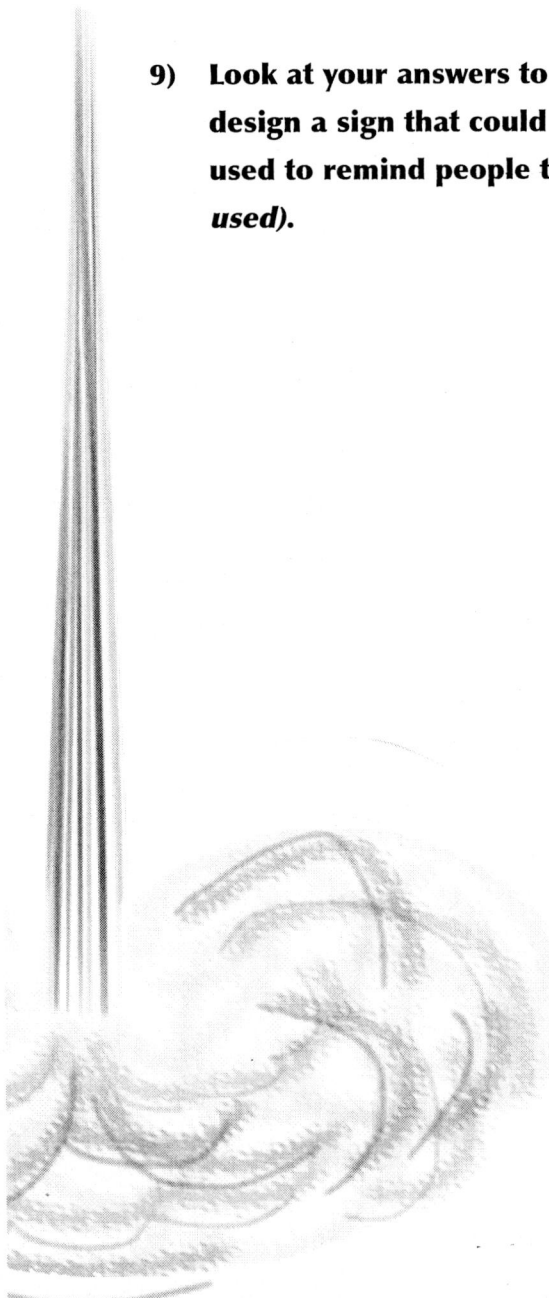

Water Supplies and Management

Global Supplies

Sadly, 20% of the world's population does not have access to clean drinking water (in other words, one in five people!) Water shortages tend to occur in poorer countries, often where there is no established system of water collection and distribution, that is, water collected in reservoirs and distributed through a network of pipes. In some parts of Africa, women and children can spend up to three hours a day walking to a source of water and queuing to fill containers. Even then, the water may be brackish or polluted.

At present, countries that don't have access to safe drinking water include:

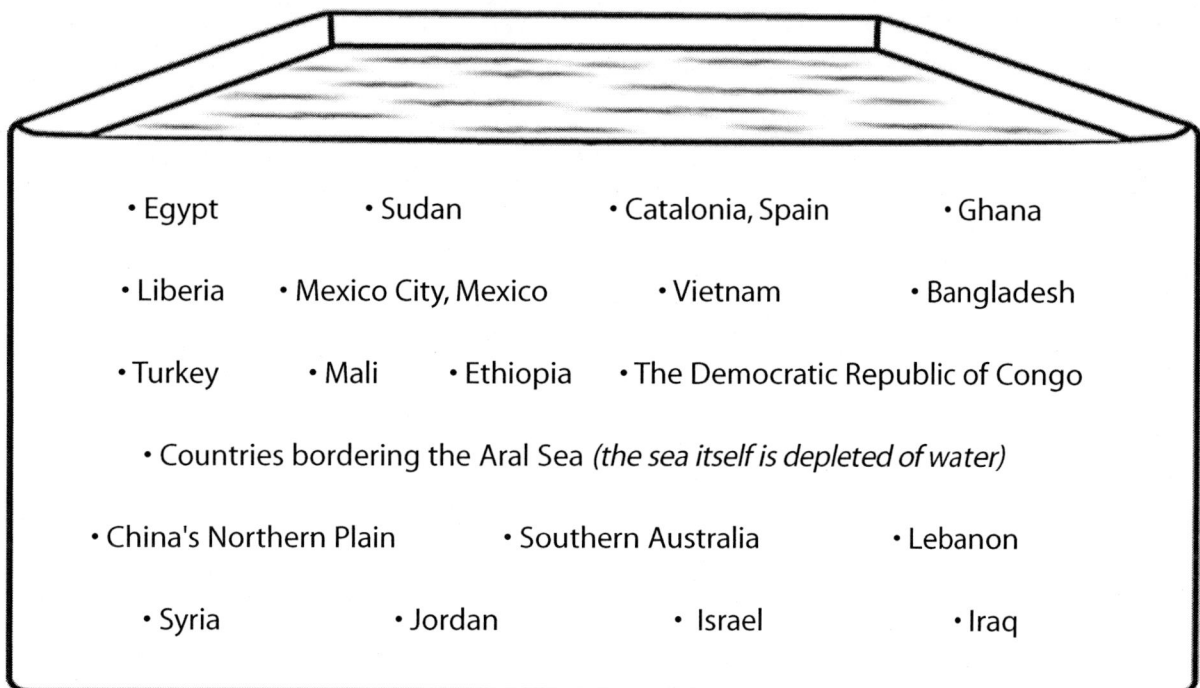

- Egypt
- Sudan
- Catalonia, Spain
- Ghana
- Liberia
- Mexico City, Mexico
- Vietnam
- Bangladesh
- Turkey
- Mali
- Ethiopia
- The Democratic Republic of Congo
- Countries bordering the Aral Sea (the sea itself is depleted of water)
- China's Northern Plain
- Southern Australia
- Lebanon
- Syria
- Jordan
- Israel
- Iraq

1) **Plot these regions on a world map.**

2) **Can you identify a link between any of them, apart from their lack of clean water?**

3) **Try to find out more about the problems facing the Aral Sea.**

The list of countries that don't have access to safe drinking water is likely to increase dramatically over the next twenty years, as the world's population increases along with the demand for fresh drinking water. It has even been suggested that the problem could lead to future wars as countries try to secure water supplies. Tension already exists in some places, where dams have been built upstream of rivers flowing through other countries, thereby reducing their supplies.

Depleting Water Supplies

Many water supplies come from deep below the earth in what are known as *aquifers*. These are areas of porous rock that act like a sponge and hold supplies of fresh water. Bore holes are sunk to reach the water. However, these natural reservoirs are becoming depleted as too much water is being taken from the ground, or bore holes have had to be sunk much deeper in order to reach the *water table*. In some places, such as California, USA, the ground on the surface has subsided, and it has been necessary to limit water extraction.

Supplies in Britain

The problem of supplying water in the British Isles is that demand is constantly growing, water supplies are limited, and they are not evenly distributed. Often, in fact, the places that have the most rainfall have the least demand for water, while the areas of greatest population density are in the driest regions.

The ten water authorities in England and Wales are responsible for managing our water supplies to ensure we have enough for our needs. During periods of drought they may transfer water from one area to another; however, so far there is no 'national grid` of pipelines like the one used to supply electricity that would enable water to be transferred from one place to another via a complete system.

4)   **What are the three problems with supplying water in Britain?**
5)   **Are there any similarities with the problems in other countries?**
6)   **How might the problems in Britain be solved?**

Water Supplies

Word Search

Use the clues below to fill in the word search. Each name is connected with water supplies. Your aim is also to find the Key Word which runs down the puzzle.

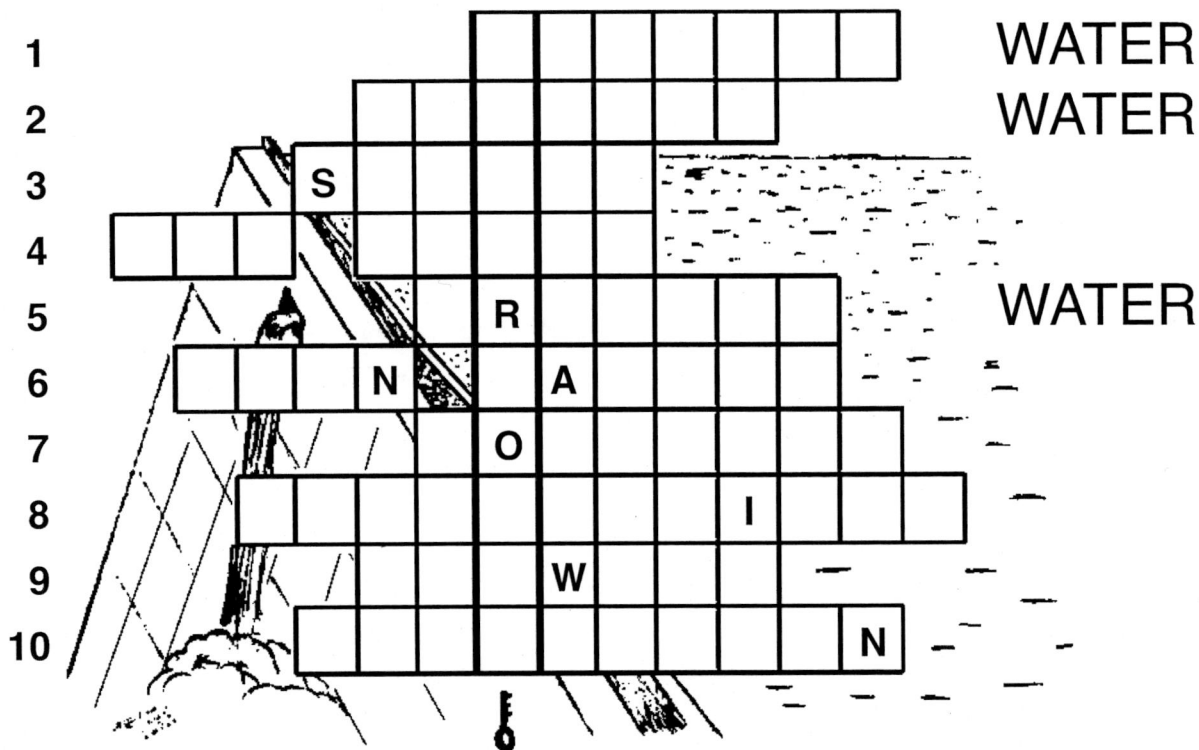

1) **In the county of the same name, between Leicester and Peterborough.**

2) **The largest man-made lake in Britain is found in Northumberland.**

3) **South-east of Number 4, and north of Balderhead Reservoir in County Durham.**

4) **Agricultural lake in the Pennines, fed by the headwaters of the River Tees.**

5) **Found at 52° 19' N, 0° 20'W.**

6) **In the Cambrian Mountains in Wales.**

7) **In Devon to supply the South West.**

8) **Not far from Brentwood in Essex.**

9) **In the Peak District near Sheffield.**

10) **North west of Derby.**

Inputs and Outputs

In the diagram below the watering can represents a reservoir, with water flowing into it (inputs) and out of it (outputs).

Decide whether the following are inputs or outputs and write the letters for each one in the correct raindrops:

(a) Hail

(b) Waste water from a sink

(c) Sprinklers on a cricket pitch

(d) Rainwater from a roof

(e) Sewage outfall

(f) A car wash

(g) Snow-melt on a mountainside

(h) Waste water from a washing machine

(i) Sleet

(j) Rainfall

Inputs

Outputs

RESERVOIR

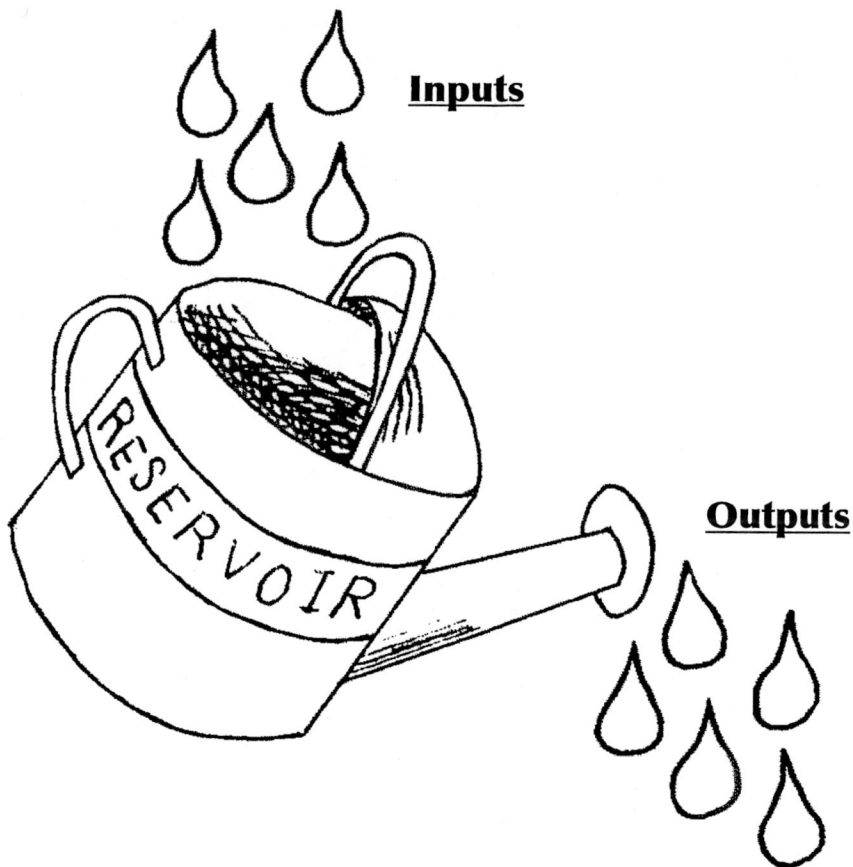

Of course, there is a danger that the amount of water used (the outputs) will exceed (be greater than) the supply (the inputs). This would create a water shortage. **What can be done to prevent this happening?**

Case Study: **Local Uses**
(Geographical Inquiry or Fieldwork)

Try to produce your own case study based on a local consumer (user), such as the fire brigade, a dairy, brewery, paper mill, bottling plant, farm etc.

Many larger companies and organisations have an Education Officer or Public Relations Department who may be able to answer your questions or arrange a visit to their premises. Alternatively, try accessing their website or e-mailing them.

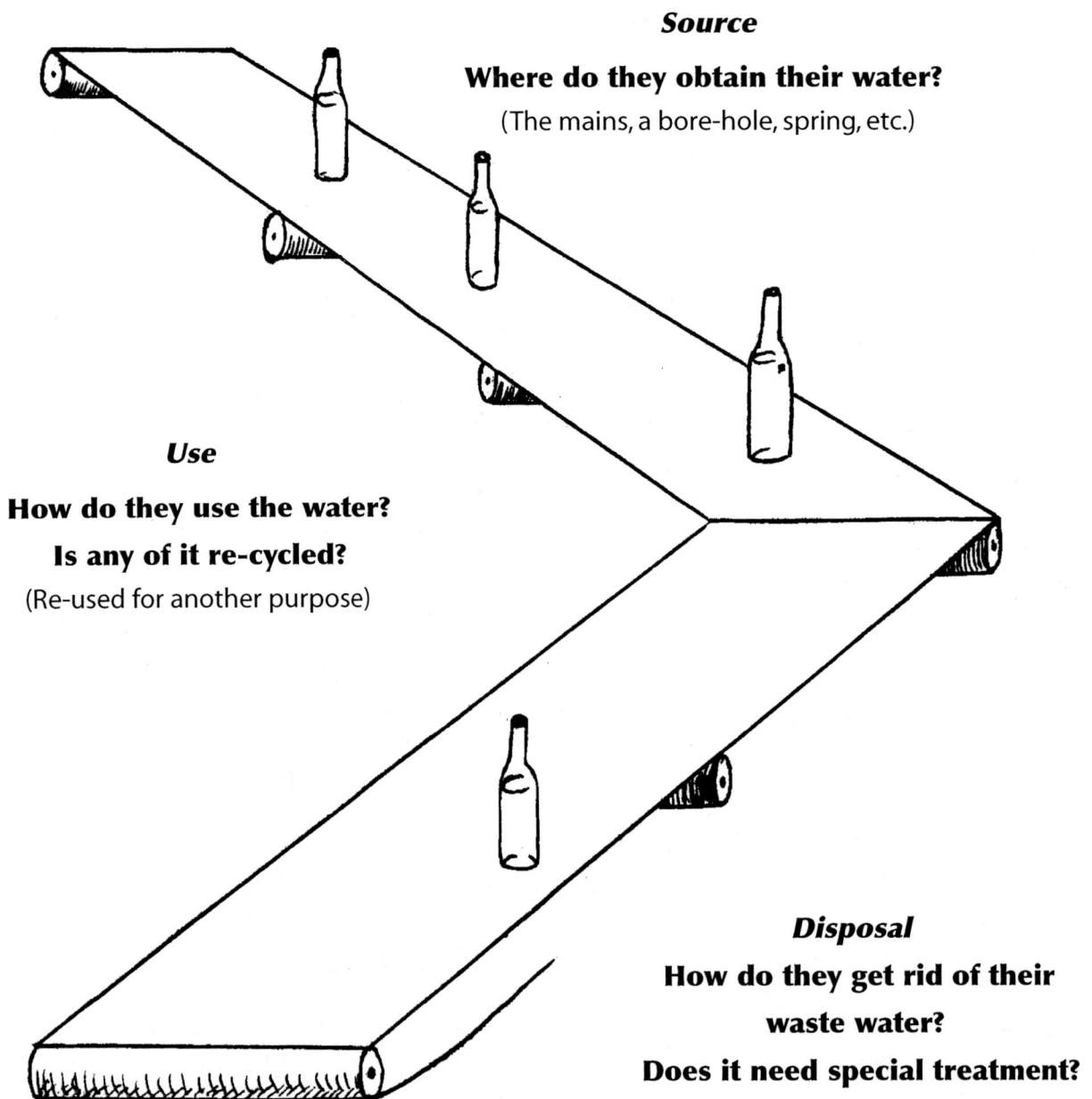

Source

Where do they obtain their water?

(The mains, a bore-hole, spring, etc.)

Use

How do they use the water?

Is any of it re-cycled?

(Re-used for another purpose)

Disposal

How do they get rid of their waste water?

Does it need special treatment?

30

WATER CONSUMPTION

DATE	DAY	USE	ESTIMATED QUANTITY

Chapter Three

Water Treatment

Why Treat Water?

In Britain, water extracted from rivers or reservoirs goes through a range of treatment processes before it reaches our taps. This ensures that it is clean and safe to drink. From the reservoir water flows to a water treatment works where it undergoes physical and chemical processes before it is allowed to join the water mains. The stages are as follows:

Screening

In this initial stage metal grids act like large sieves to remove floating debris such as leaves and twigs.

Flocculation

As the water flows through large tanks, chemicals are added. These include small quantities of aluminium sulphate or iron sulphate which acts as a coagulant, causing impurities such as bacteria and tiny particles of dirt to be caught in a dense layer of what is known as floc.

Clarification

The floc has to be separated from the 'clarified' water. *This can be done in two ways:*

(a) Sedimentation

The water is allowed to settle beneath the floc, and can then be drawn off.

(b) Dissolved Air Flotation

Millions of small bubbles of air are introduced from the bottom of the collecting tank. These force the floc to the surface where it can be scraped off mechanically using brushes.

Filtration

The clarified water is now passed through a series of filters made up of a bed of fine sand to remove any traces of coagulant or particles.

Chlorination

Small quantities of chlorine are added to kill any remaining bacteria, and also as an aid to dental well-being. (This stage has been open to controversy in recent years.)

Water Stabilisation

Sometimes a solution of lime is added to help protect the water mains from corrosion.

Sampling

The water quality is constantly monitored. Samples are taken at various stages during and after the treatment process, and analysed in laboratories to ensure that it is safe to drink.

S **1) Make up a flow diagram to illustrate the process of water treatment.**

2) Try to find out more about chlorination and what the advantages (good points) and disadvantages (bad points) of this stage may be.

Natural Mineral Water

Some people prefer to drink bottled water which is not subject to the same treatment as tap water. This has to meet certain high standards; it must be bottled at its source, and no chemical or bacterial treatment is permitted. As it is pure and **unadulterated** (nothing is added to it), natural mineral water may contain different levels of dissolved mineral salts and have a slightly different taste, depending on its origins.

Other types of water are also available:

Spring Water

This is bottled from a single underground source, but as it does not have to conform to Natural Mineral Water Regulations it may be treated.

Spa Water

This is said to have therapeutic qualities (i.e. it is thought to be good for one's health), although that does not mean it is always pleasant to drink!

Carbonated Water

Due to the geology, British mineral waters are Still. To create a sparkling variety the water is injected with carbon dioxide during bottling, so that it appears like lemonade.

Table Water

This label can be applied to any water, including tap water, which is treated and bottled.

D 3) **Look in shops and supermarkets for examples of different types of bottled water. Notice how their chemical composition may vary depending upon their source.**

Case Study: Buxton Natural Mineral Water

The spa town of Buxton was built around the mineral water springs in the Peak District of Derbyshire. Water from its catchment area to the east and south-east of the town flows down through a fissured limestone aquifer. Above this is a layer of volcanic lava which acts as a cap, protecting the water from surface contamination. The clear, mountain water rises from a depth of 1,500 metres through faults to the town above. 768,000 litres a day emerges, at a constant temperature of 27.5°C. According to the British Geological Survey, this water originally fell as rain over five thousand years ago.

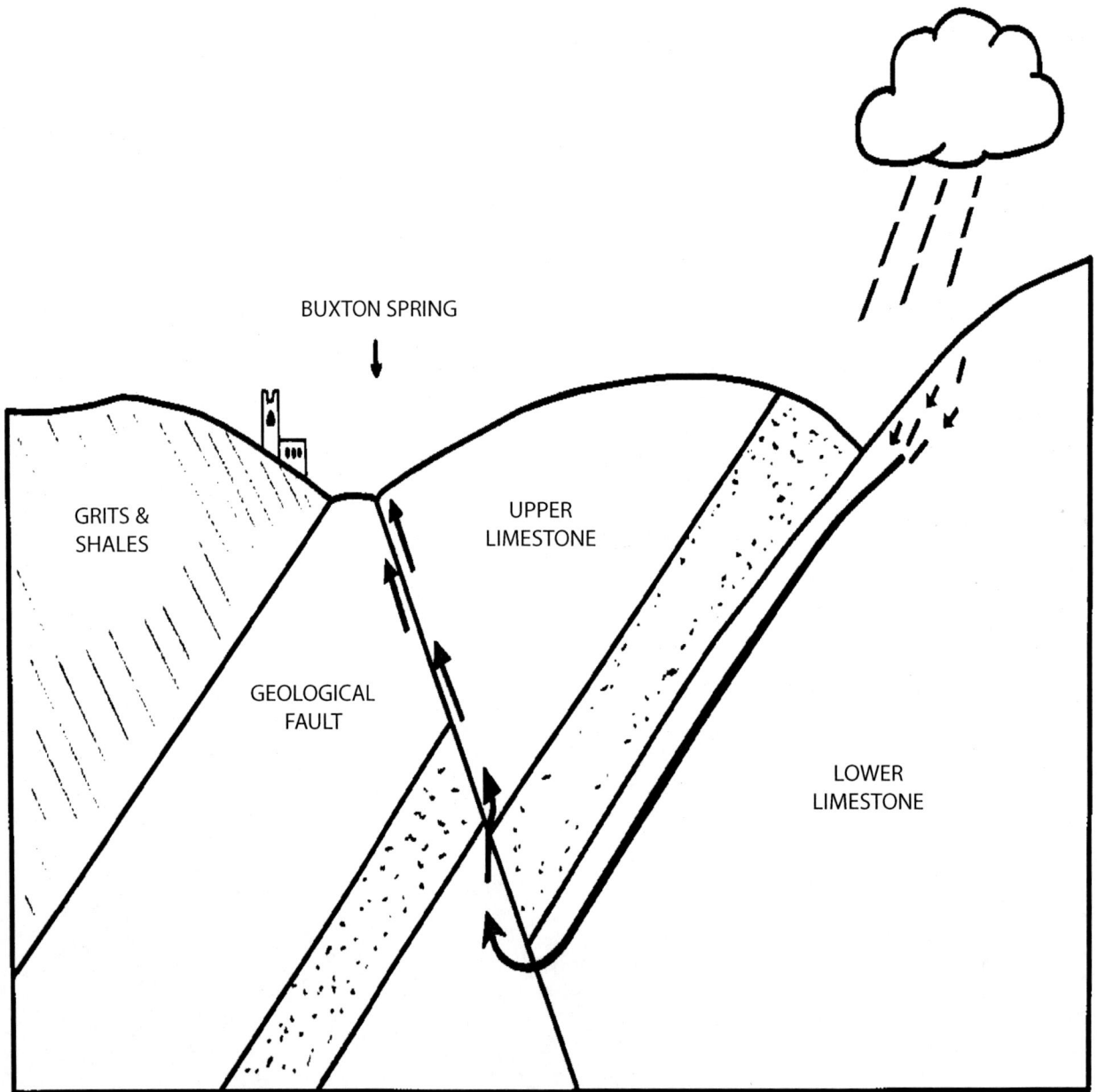

BUXTON SPRING

GRITS & SHALES

UPPER LIMESTONE

GEOLOGICAL FAULT

LOWER LIMESTONE

History

The Buxton springs were discovered by the Romans in 79 AD. They believed the water to have health benefits and named the area Aquae Arnemetiae - The Spa of the Goddess of the Grove. During the sixteenth-century Mary Queen of Scots was a regular visitor to the baths of the town. Since that time visitors, both rich and poor, famous and obscure, have continued to take the waters.

Bottling the Water

Water from Buxton was first bottled in the mid-nineteenth century. Today Buxton Natural Mineral Water is a subsidiary of Perrier Vittel UK Ltd., which is part of Nestlé. The town of Buxton retains the sole rights to the source, which is leased to the company. Following the construction of a £3.8 million extension of the bottling plant in 1995, production increased by 40 million bottles a year. It has a total annual bottling capacity of 90 million bottles, and demand continues to grow.

Other Waters Include:

Perrier Its source is at Vergèze, near Nîmes in the south of France. It is the leading sparkling water brand, its bubbles formed by natural gas found in the rock strata below the spring.

Vitel Its source is in the Vosges Mountains of north-eastern France. Vitel's water is said to have therapeutic benefits.

Ashbourne Like Buxton, Ashbourne is in Derbyshire, on the edge of the Peak District National Park. It is the house water of several leading hotel groups, and is widely distributed within the catering market.

Volvic This comes from the Auvergne National Park in central France. Fresh rain water is naturally filtered through many layers of volcanic rock and sand. It is drawn from a huge aquifer and bottled immediately.

S **4)** **Make up a table to compare the advantages and disadvantages of tap water and bottled water.**

D **5)** **Should all tap water go through the same treatment processes, regardless of how it is used? What are the alternatives to this uniform treatment policy?**

Sewage Treatment

Sewage is any waste product from a sink, bath or toilet. About 99.5% of this is water, and is transported to the treatment works through the sewers by gravity. It is vital that waste is treated properly before it is returned to the water cycle.

Firstly solids are removed during preliminary treatment; such things as paper, rags or twigs, as well as sand and grit that could damage pumps are physically extracted. Then **primary treatment** sees the remaining solids (the poo!) separated from the liquids in settling tanks. This is then known as sludge, and is used as a fertiliser on farms after further treatment.

During the **secondary treatment** a biological process using naturally occurring micro-organisms that feed on the bacteria in the sewage purifies the remaining liquid. This occurs in aeration tanks in which air is introduced to speed up the process. Before the water is released it may go through tertiary treatment, using a final range of filters consisting of reed beds or sand, or by allowing the water to pass ultra-violet light which kills any remaining bacteria.

Many water companies will organise educational visits to water treatment works. This could be combined with a trip to a local reservoir to take advantage of leisure activities such as fishing, wind surfing or canoeing that are often provided.

Chapter Four

Floods and Flood Prevention

Floods and Flood Prevention

Floods may be *expected* and welcomed, for they provide irrigation and fertile alluvial soil *(for example, the River Nile)*, or **unexpected** and harmful.

Three quarters of the world's fresh water is held as ice, so as Global Warming increases, flooding is likely to become a more common occurrence. It has been estimated that it could happen as frequently as every ten years. In Britain the south-east coast is particularly at risk.

The Impacts of Flooding

Try to fill in the missing letters:

Negative Aspects

• B_____ can be damaged as the interiors are covered with mud, or the f_____ could be undermined.

• On farms c_____ may be ruined and a_____ could be washed away or need rescuing.

• Economic - Home owners, insurance companies or governments have to p_____ to put right the damage.

• Transport systems may be disrupted as r_____ and r_____ tracks may be impassable or damaged.

• Water supplies can be damaged or con_____ with sewage. This could lead to dis_____ such as cholera.

• People may have to be put into temporary acc_____ or even re-housed.

Positive Aspects

- Floods deposit fertile soil, such as the annual floods on the River Nile.

- Floods wash away any pollutants.

- Floods replenish ground water.

Flood Prevention

(a) River channels can be widened and deepened.

(b) Embankments may be built along river banks to contain the rising water.

(c) Barrages or temporary dams could be constructed, such as the Thames Barrier.

(d) Flood relief channels can drain low-lying land.

(e) Dykes are often built to protect reclaimed land, e.g. The Netherlands.

(f) Holding reservoirs can be created to store surplus water.

The Thames Barrier was constructed between 1974 and 1982 to protect London from flooding. This will become more frequent as sea levels rise, and the area is slowly sinking so is more likely to suffer during high tides. Once raised, the four main gates are as high as a five-storey building. To date they have been needed on 88 occasions.

Examples of Floods

- In 1887 the Hwang-Ho (Yellow River) in China burst its banks, killing 900,000 people.

- On 16 and 17 May 1943, during the Second World War, the 'Dambusters' attacked the Möhne and Eder Dams in an attempt to disrupt German factories.

- In 1952 in Lynmouth, Devon, 34 people died in floods. Heavy rain fell over Exmoor and was channelled down the narrow valleys of the East and West Lyn rivers which met at Lynmouth.

- In 1959 the Malpasset Dam in Frejus, France, burst. The resulting flood killed over 500 people. It failed because it was built on a rock called schist, which cracks easily.

- On 16 August 2004 Boscastle in Cornwall was devastated by a flash flood. (See Case Study page 48)

- On 26 December 2004 a tsunami struck coastal regions in the Indian Ocean following an earthquake beneath the sea off the coast of Sumatra. About 150,000 people were killed in eleven countries as the waves swept across low-lying coastal areas and thousands of isolated islands, while over a million were left homeless, and without access to fresh water, food, or medical supplies. (See Case Study, Chapter 8, page 78)

Fill in the table below using the details on this page, or by adding other information you might find:

Examples of Floods			
Date	**Place**	**Number Killed**	**Cause**
1887			
1943			
1953	*East coast of England*	*Over 300*	
1959			
Aug. 2004	*Boscastle, Cornwall*	*0*	
Dec. 2004			*Tsunami*

Case Study: **Flash Flood, Boscastle, Cornwall**

Localised weather conditions were the cause of flash floods which swept through the village of Boscastle on the north coast of Cornwall on 16 August 2004. It is believed that 20 days' worth of rain fell upon high ground in just two hours. Water surged down the rivers that ran through the centre of the village and into the harbour. In a short space of time flood water rose to three metres in depth and swept away cars, uprooted trees and tore up roads, bridges and embankments. Witnesses reported seeing a caravan and two cars being washed over the top of a bridge. "To see a mobile home go by like a cork bobbing on the water was just unbelievable," another one said. Almost a hundred vehicles were swept from the roads and car park, through the main street, and out into the harbour or open sea, while six buildings collapsed as water raced through them.

The water rose so quickly that some people, many of whom were on holiday, were forced to climb to attics, rooftops or up trees to escape. Seven RAF helicopters, as well as two private ones, were involved in the rescue operation which winched around 120 people from the tops of buildings, upstairs windows and trees. One baby was winched to safety in a rucksack.

As the flood water receded, it became clear the village was devastated. A sea of mud covered everything, inside and out. Cars lay crumpled, half buried, some upside down. Large trees lay like broken match sticks. Personal possessions - fridges, crockery, tables, toys - stuck out from the mud.

Being the middle of the holiday season, the normal population of 800 people in this popular and picturesque seaside village had been swollen by visitors. Around 50 tourists were given temporary accommodation in a rescue base set up in a nearby leisure centre. Here they were provided with food, blankets, sleeping bags and clean clothes. As many had lost their cars, arrangements had to be made for them to get home. Some 33 pets, including dogs, cats, one cockatiel, five canaries, two hamsters and a pet rat, were rescued and had to be re-united with their anxious owners.

Miraculously, no-one appears to have died in the flash flood. Some time later a pile of shoes from a shop in Boscastle was washed up on the beach at Westward Ho! about 65 km. away!

The Causes

An air mass sweeping in from the Atlantic Ocean converged with an air mass inland. When they met over the high land of Bodmin Moor the air was forced to rise, condensing rapidly and causing heavy rain. This flowed down the narrow valleys which converged at Boscastle and neighbouring valleys. The problem was compounded by the high tide, so that the water could not escape so easily to the sea.

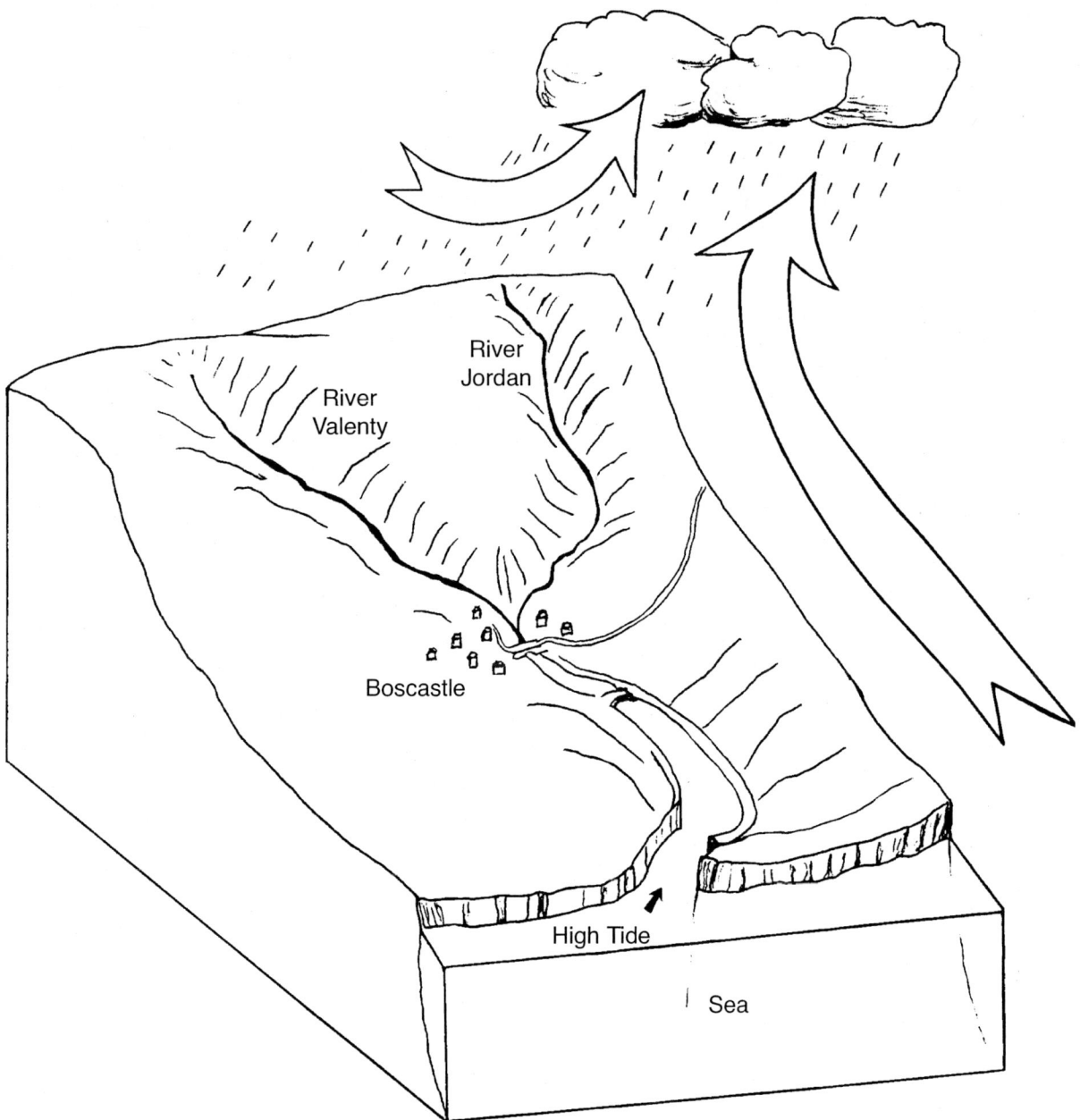

~~~ 1) Use the information from the Case Study to write a newspaper report on the flood. You may like to write it from the point of view of a visitor, a helicopter winch man, or one of the fire brigade involved in the rescue operation.

S 2) Divide the information into *causes* and *effects*.

Flood Simulation

3) Use Figure 7, Chapter 1, for the following:

    (a) Using a suitable colour, mark on any land that would be flooded if the water level rose to 50 metres above sea level.

D

    (b) What effect would this have on man's activities in this area?

    (c) Mark on to Figure 7 any methods you would use to prevent flooding in the future. (Use the Flood Prevention section above to help you if necessary.)

Chapter Five

Droughts and Deserts

Many parts of the world are beginning to feel the effect of Global Warming. Deserts are growing larger (desertification) as land that was once savanna grassland is unable to survive increasingly harsh conditions and is encroached upon by the neighbouring desert. Parts of Sudan and Ethiopia which were until recently able to sustain people and herds of cattle have become a barren wilderness, leading to migration or starvation. In such places the search for water is of paramount importance.

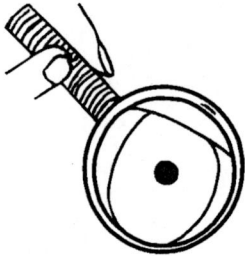

The Search for Water

There are several methods of searching for new water supplies. These range from the simple yet mysterious, to the technical and complicated.

Dousing

Some people appear to have a natural ability to detect water beneath the ground, be it an existing pipe or a new supply, by just using a forked stick or dousing rods. Doubters regard it as little more than poppycock, yet it appears to work: those with this innate ability often have to fight the force felt in their wrists when water is present.

Sinking Bore-Holes

If a site is suspected of containing water, either through dousing, or because of favourable geology, an exploratory bore-hole may be sunk using a small drilling rig. Should an aquifer be detected, water will often rise up as a strong jet until it is capped.

Obtaining Water from the Ground

In More Economically Developed Countries (M.E.D.C.s) electric pumps are used to raise water. In other countries hand-operated pumps may be available, otherwise water may have to be raised at a well, or by using a simple water-lifting devise, such as the Egyptian *shaduf*. This is a lever with a bucket at one end and a counter-weight at the other.

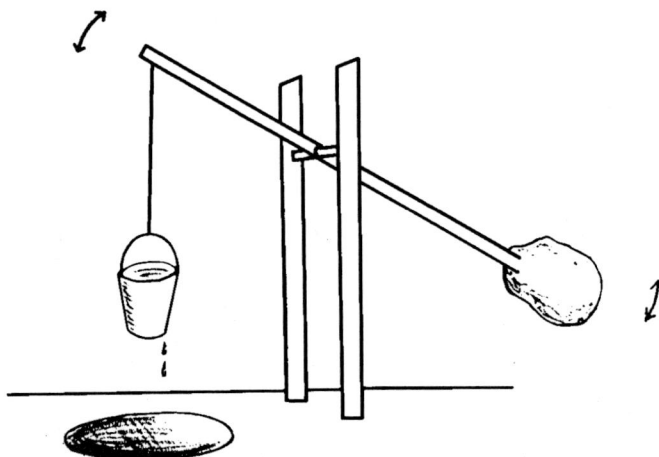

Another method is to use an artesian well, which uses the pressure of water below the ground to force a stream to the surface via a bore hole. If the pressure is insufficient or drops then a suction pump may be needed.

Try your hand at dousing. You never know, you may be a natural... All you will need are the cases of two old biro pens and two pieces of bent wire, such as from an old wire coat hanger. Following the diagram below, place each piece of wire in each pen tube. Then lightly hold the tubes in each hand, with the wire pointing forward and able to rotate. Walk slowly across the playground or where you know there is a water pipe below the ground. If you have the knack the two pieces of wire should swing together when you cross water.

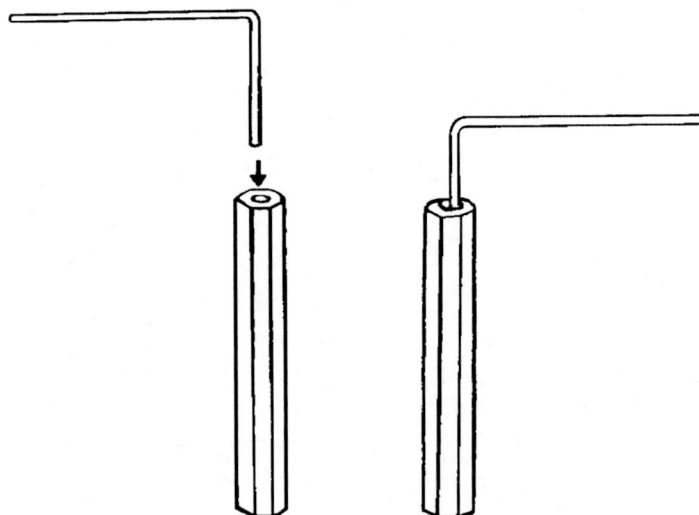

Why not build a working model of an Egyptian shaduf? Follow the instructions below.

1)

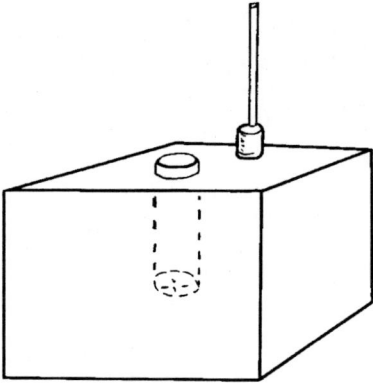

Take a cardboard box for a base. Insert half a plastic bottle into one end to form the well. An old pencil or dowel serves as an upright, supported by a cotton reel.

2) Cut a T-shaped piece of card (A) that is the pivot. It should be long enough to rest on the cotton reel. Bend it round the upright and secure it with glue and a paper fastener. A second piece of card (B) serves as a 'saddle' for the beam.

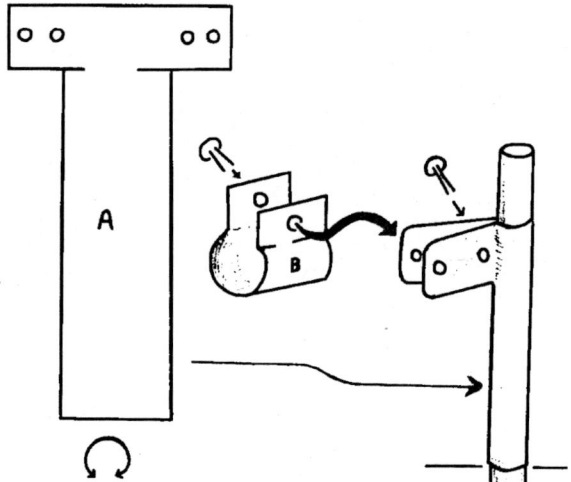

A

B

3) Use a plastic bottle top for a bucket. Carefully make a hole in either side, then use a piece of wire for a handle. Your bucket may need a plasticine weight on one side so it will fill with water.

4)

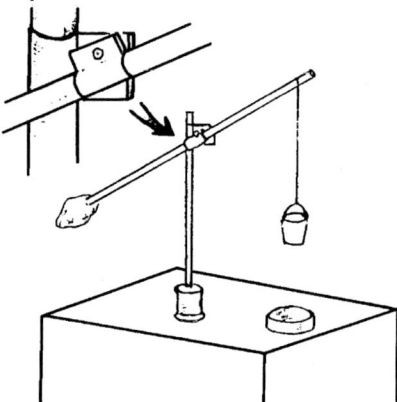

Assemble the shaduf, using a wooden skewer or dowel for a beam. Attach the saddle with glue and suspend it from the card pivot with a paper fastener. A lump of plasticine serves as a counter-weight. Carefully fill the well with water and try it out. You may like to use papier-mâché to turn the box into a hill.

Collecting rain water so that it can be re-used is known as water harvesting. Various methods can be used:

(a) A water butt can be supplied by a connection to a gutter downpipe.

(b) Water can be channelled into a small underground storage reservoir. This has the advantage of reducing the amount lost through evaporation. The design of new buildings could include this feature.

Design a water harvester for your school. The water would not be safe to drink, but could be used for flushing toilets or watering plants.

Case Study: Watering the Desert - The Al Hidd Desalination Plant, Bahrain

～～ 1) Use an atlas to find Bahrain. The index will tell you:

(a) The latitude -

(b) The longitude -

(c) The capital - Manama

(d) Area - 717 square k.m. (277 sq. miles)

Find out:

(e) The sea it faces is -

(f) Its large neighbour to the west is -

(g) The climate of the area -

Bahrain is an archipelago made up of some 30 islands. The name Bahrain means 'two seas`. It was able to boost its economy by being one of the first countries in the region to discover oil and build a refinery. The country changed its status from being an emirate to a constitutional monarchy in February 2002, and also in that year elections were held for a 40-member parliament, the Council of Deputies. The present king, Sheikh Hamad, was educated in England and trained in the US Army.

Demand for both power and water has increased so much in Bahrain that the government decided to build a new power and desalination plant on Muharraq Island. Desalination is a process that changes sea water into fresh water. The scheme cost $360 million, and was carried out by an American engineering and construction company.

The first phase of the project saw the building of a new gas-fired power plant. The second phase was to replace the old desalination plant. This had treated brackish (salty) ground water, but the level in the aquifer had dropped and the ground water supply could have run out within four years had nothing been done. The new plant treats sea water, converting 30 million gallons a day into fresh water through a 'multistage flash process`.

As well as the desalination plant, blending stations were also constructed where water could be stored in huge steel tanks before being pumped to other areas. Some 45 km of water mains were installed and existing facilities upgraded to deal with the increased capacity.

Desalination plants are expensive to run, but are becoming increasingly important in arid regions. A similar scheme was recently completed at Fujairah in the United Arab Emirates.

2) **What is meant by desalination?**

3) **How much did the Al Hidd Desalination Plant cost?**

4) **The old plant extracted water from an underground aquifer. However, sea water had found its way into this natural reservoir. What other problem existed with this supply?**

5) **How much fresh water a day can be produced?**

6) **Besides the desalination plant itself, what other equipment was needed?**

Try your own desalination in a science lesson. Take a container of water and add a quantity of table salt to it. Boil the water and allow the steam to condense into a container. This is your fresh water.

(a) **Can you think of any problems with this process?**

(b) **What by-product are you left with?**

Chapter Six

Water Pollution

Pollution means to contaminate something with a harmful substance. Water pollution can take many forms and have many causes. Until recently, rivers, lakes and the sea provided a convenient dumping ground for all manner of waste materials.

A Global Problem

In many parts of the world, polluted water, inadequate waste disposal and poor water management lead to serious public health problems. The World Summit on Sustainable Development was held in Johannesburg, South Africa, in 2002. This highlighted the problems of water shortages and the lack of supplies of fresh water, and it was agreed to aim to halve the number of people without access to clean water or proper sanitation by 2015. At the moment it is claimed that 10,000 children die every day from cholera and other water-related diseases. Some 80% of all diseases and a third of all deaths in Less Economically Developed Countries are attributable to contaminated water. Such diseases include malaria, typhoid, salmonella, E coli and hepatitis. Bilharzia is carried by snails that live in rivers, while Guinea Worm Disease, which cripples its victims, is transmitted to others when the worm releases millions of larvae into the water from a person already affected.

Simple, yet effective methods do exist to combat such diseases. Parasitic diseases such as these can be almost eliminated by using a simple nylon filter in the water supply. It was found that in Nepal, which has plentiful supplies of water, rivers were being polluted by poor sanitation arrangements. A solution was to pipe water from closer to its source, where it was still pure.

1) **What are some causes of water pollution?**

2) **How many children become victims of water-borne diseases?**

3) **Where has the best place been found to extract water in mountainous areas?**

4) **Try to find out more about some of the diseases mentioned, and how they are linked to polluted water.**

A National Problem

As an industrialised nation, Britain's water pollution problems are somewhat different, but they still exist. Pollution can enter rivers and streams in a variety of ways. *Industries* may still, unwittingly, pollute local streams, and the contaminants are then carried with the water to other areas, causing the problem to spread. *Leaching* can also occur when chemicals are washed (or leached) out of a rubbish tip and find their way into a water course. *Farms* can also cause pollution through fertilisers being washed off the land and into lakes and rivers. Here tiny plants called algae feed off them. Decomposing algae can leave a green scum on the surface which depletes the oxygen levels, killing fish. Silage effluent may find its way into rivers, or run-off can carry slurry, herbicides or pesticides from farm land. This can kill fish, and other animals higher up the food chain, as well as affecting the natural balance of an *ecosystem*. During the winter months abnormal quantities of salt may be found in rivers, as road salt is washed away by the rain. Various agencies have the task of monitoring the state of our rivers and streams, and have powers to fine those who are found to be causing pollution. *Domestic* waste, such as old fridges, mattresses or litter may be dumped in streams by unscrupulous and uncaring people.

Unforeseen accidents or disasters can have a more devastating affect on the environment, such as when ships are damaged or wrecked on our coasts. It is not only the cargo that may be lost and causes pollution, but the ship's fuel oil may escape from ruptured tanks. Then major clean-up operations have to be mounted on land and sea.

5) **What types of water pollution may occur in Britain?**

6) **Which do you think would be the most easy to deal with, and why?**

7) **Does pollution matter? Why?**

8) **What is an ecosystem?**

Case Study: **The Shetlands Oil Disaster**

On 4 January 1993 the Liberian-registered tanker, *Braer*, was en route to Canada from Norway when it went aground at Garth Ness, on the south-west coast of Shetland. The vessel was carrying 85,000 tonnes of light crude oil, more than twice the quantity that was carried by the *Exxon Valdes* which devastated the coast of Alaska in 1989. The ship also had onboard 500 tonnes of fuel oil. Apart from the size and nature of her cargo, there was every reason to be concerned that it could cause an ecological disaster: the ship had gone aground near the Sumburgh Roost tidal race, which could quickly cause the oil to spread, and the waters of the Shetland islands is one of the most important wildlife areas of the North Atlantic. Sea birds that were harmed as their wings and feathers became matted with tar included the great northern diver, black guillemot, eider duck, long-tailed duck and sea cormorant. Other migratory birds, such as puffin, gannet, and razorbill would be returning to breed the following spring. Besides sea birds, other species such as seals, porpoises and killer whales, were also at risk.

The Effect on the Food Chain

Lumps of oil mix with sand which causes it to sink. It then kills bottom feeders, worms, fish and crabs. This has an impact on larger creatures that depend on them for food. After time, globules of oil escape and float upwards as little tar balls, again endangering wildlife.

The Long-term Effect

Fortunately, on this occasion, the effect was not as dramatic as first feared. Commercial salmon farms suffered for some time. However, there was no long term effect on the local cod and herring industry. Much of the oil was carried out to sea. Nature has a way of healing itself; in time the oil was dispersed, and smaller quantities were broken down by natural bacteria.

How the Oil Slick Spread

Each tide carried more oil into the shallows of the inter-tidal zone.

Further out, currents forced the oil slick to move along the coast.

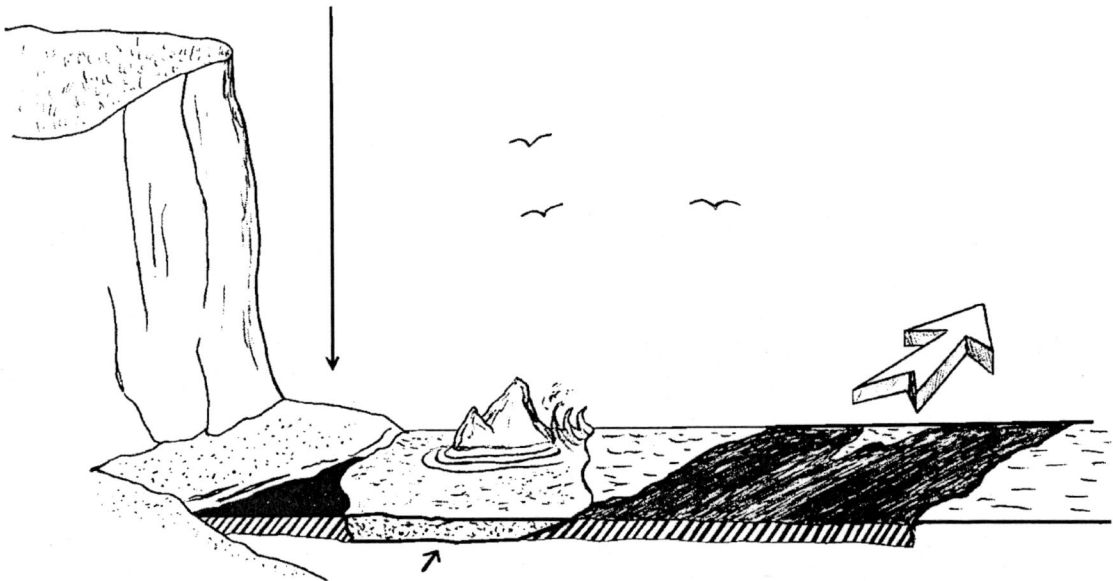

Oil and water were mixed by the wind to form a 'mousse' capable of travelling 800-900 kms.

1) **Find the Shetland Islands in an atlas. Name the capital.**

2) **How much oil did the tanker, *Braer*, carry?**

3) **Explain how the oil slick spread.**

4) **How does the oil affect the food chain?**

5) **Which (a) sea birds (b) other species, are in danger from oil slicks?**

6) **Explain why the tanker *Braer* went aground in the Shetland Islands.**

7) **Braer was registered in Liberia. Where is this? You may like to investigate why so many ships are registered in Liberia or Panama.**

8) **Try to find out more about other oil pollution incidents, such as that caused by the *Exxon Valdes*, mentioned above.**

D How could you mount a campaign to stop a particular industry from polluting the environment? (Consider a factory making, perhaps, surf boards, training shoes, cosmetics, or paints. Think about who you would need to convince that their production methods were wrong, and how could you persuade them to change their ways?)

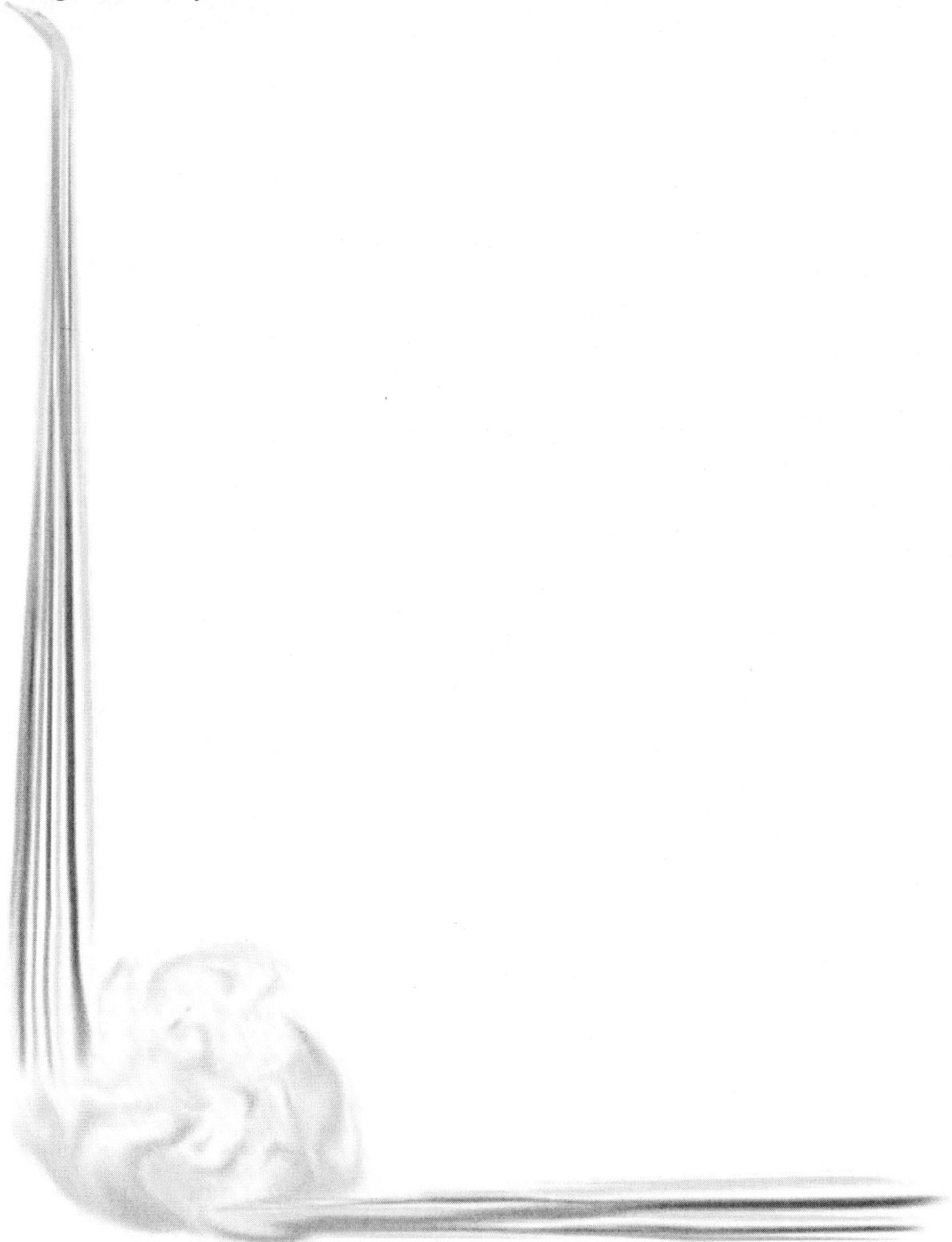

Chapter Seven

Water for Agriculture, Industry and Power

Agriculture

At a global level, agriculture is the largest consumer of water, with 70 to 80% being used to irrigate fields. Unfortunately, as has been seen, rainfall does not always occur where it is needed. The answer then is to provide irrigation. However, unless the water goes directly to where it is wanted it is wasted. It has been estimated that only about 40% of all *irrigation* water actually gets to where it is required. The rest evaporates or drains away - imagine traditional sprinklers that throw large volumes of water into the air. One solution to this problem has been to use drip irrigation (or trickle irrigation) which provides the plants with water through plastic piping directly to where it is needed. This provides a saving of about 70% and has been used successfully in semi-arid regions such as Spain, California, Israel and South Africa.

Industry

At present, industry uses some 14% of the water taken out of rivers and reservoirs, not including that used as cooling water in power stations, etc. It is widely used as part of various manufacturing processes, as well as in food production and packaging. During the nineteenth century, and before the advent of the railways, Britain's extensive canal system was vital for the transport of raw materials and goods.

Water Power - Historical Links

Tide mills were used in Britain before 1100 A.D. Ponds were constructed by the side of estuaries. These were filled by the incoming tide, then the water was released to power under-shot water wheels. However, this infinite and environmentally friendly idea died out.

Water Power

P A S T	*Water Mills* Undershot	For centuries water wheels were used to drive machinery. They are still used in some L.E.D.C's such as Egypt or India.	**Study the information on this page. Can you work out how the water is used in each example? E.g. the weight of water, its movement or temperature.**
P R E S E N T	*Hydro-Electric Power (H.E.P)*		*Geothermal*
	Water in a reservoir (1) is held back by a dam (2). It is allowed to flow through pipes (penstocks) (3) to turn turbines (4). These drive generators (5) which produce the electricity.		Svartsengi geothermal power station near Reykjavik in Iceland uses the heat of hot volcanic rock to provide hot water to 85% of the population. Uncontrolled, it would rise as spectacular columns of boiling water called geysers.
F U T U R E	*Tidal Power* Tide		*Wave Power*
	The rise and fall of the tide could be used to power generators, particularly where the tidal range is high. (See Case Study, page 71).		The movement of the waves could be harnessed to produce electricity. 'Nodding ducks' and the 'Cockerell raft' have been recent attempts.

Using any of the four maps below, mark on places you think would be suitable for producing water power. (You may wish to add cities which would use that power.)

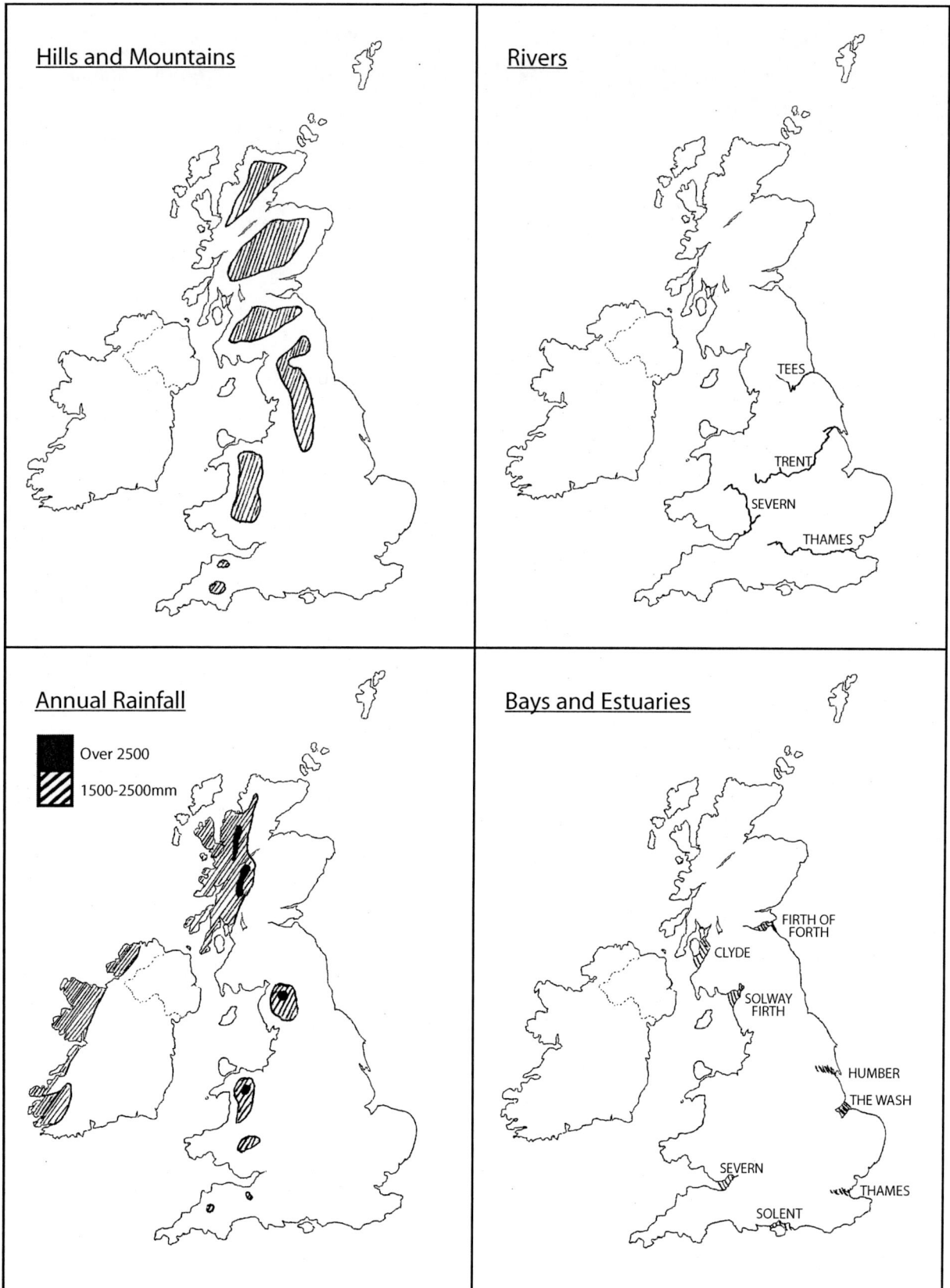

Hills and Mountains

Rivers

TEES

TRENT

SEVERN

THAMES

Annual Rainfall

■ Over 2500

▧ 1500-2500mm

Bays and Estuaries

FIRTH OF FORTH

CLYDE

SOLWAY FIRTH

HUMBER

THE WASH

SEVERN

THAMES

SOLENT

Water Power Today

The most successful method of producing power from water at the moment is through hydro-electric power. A steady flow of water is directed through a series of turbines which are used to drive electricity generators. However, the downside of this seemingly ideal power source is that such schemes have to be located in areas of high rainfall, and these are often remote from centres of population.

As man's energy needs grow, along with the desire to find alternatives to fossil fuels, experiments continue into other forms of water power. In future a large proportion of our energy requirements may be met by off-shore wave or tidal power generators.

Tea Break

Case Study: Seaflow Sea Turbine

The world's only underwater tidal turbine is presently undergoing tests off the coast of north Devon. If it is successful it will lead to larger schemes being developed at other suitable locations around the UK and help fulfil the government's targets of producing 545 megawatts of renewable energy by 2010.

An 11-metre-wide, single-rotor turbine, that looks like an aeroplane's propeller, is mounted on a steel column which is set into a socket drilled into the sea bed. It is turned by the flow of water in a similar way to a windmill being driven by the wind, but will be more efficient, as the tides are more predictable and less variable. This 18-tonne prototype should be capable of producing 300 kilowatts of electricity - enough to power 200 homes. If it proves successful, commercial twin-turbine units will be created.

This test project, which has cost £3.5 million, has been located about a mile off Forepoint, near Lynmouth in Devon, at what is considered to be a high-energy marine site. The platform can be seen from the shore, but despite initial concerns about the visual impact of the turbine, most people have accepted it, and consider it could even attract holiday makers to the area who might wish to see history in the making.

Imagine you work for an advertising agency that has been given the task of selling the idea of tidal turbines commercially.

- **What arguments would you put forward to promote the scheme?**

- **What are the objections that might be raised against the idea?**

- **Conduct a class questionnaire to gauge the popularity of different types of water power.**

- **Which is the most popular and why?**

Chapter Eight

Global Issues

Case Study: The Three Gorges Scheme on the Yangtze River, China

The Yangtze River is China's longest river, and at 6,300 km. in length ranks as the world's third longest river, as well as having over 700 other rivers joining it. From its headwaters in the Tibetan Plateau it flows east, irrigating one of the country's chief rice-growing areas, before entering the East China Sea near Shanghai. Some of China's greatest cities stand on its banks. It passes through eight provinces and divides the north of the country from the south.

A 193 km. stretch flows through steep limestone cliffs and is known as *The Three Gorges*. It is here that a huge dam is being built to provide hydro-electric power. China's economy is growing rapidly; one only has to consider the amount of our consumer goods that is now produced there. The Three Gorges Scheme will go some way towards meeting China's energy needs, as well as reducing the country's dependence on fossil fuels. The dam is located at Sandouping, and when completed in 2009 it will be 2 km. long and 185 metres high, making it the largest dam in the world. It will hold back a 600 km. long reservoir that will be up to 176 metres deep. Hydro-electric power (H.E.P.) will be produced by 26 turbines. The dam will also control what has been historically a dangerous and treacherous stretch of river and make water-borne trade easier.

During its construction 22 water diversion holes allowed the river to flow through the huge structure. Once completed, on 1 June 2003 they were closed and the reservoir began to fill up. To allow shipping to pass five shiplocks were included on the left bank, as well as a ship lift.

Despite its amazing statistics, the scheme has not been without its critics. Many fear it could become the focus of terrorist attacks. Others are concerned about the environmental impact. The spectacular landscape of precipitous gorges will be gone for ever. Also, it has been estimated that one billion tons of sewage will flow into the reservoir each year, creating an ecological disaster.

The five-stage permanent ship lock at the Three Gorges Dam.

The Three Gorges Fact File

〰 **Try to use a variety of resources, such as an atlas, the Internet, travel brochures and text books to fill in the following information. Please note - you may find different figures in various web sites. The Chinese statistics tend to be optimistic, the American sites are largely against the scheme and are pessimistic.**

1. Latitude:

2. Longitude:

3. Number of dams:

4. The cost of the project:

5. The number of people to be re-housed:

6. The number of cities submerged:

7. The number of towns submerged:

8. The number of villages submerged:

9. The area to be submerged:

10. The amount of rock removed:

11. The amount of power to be produced:

12. The effect on (a) navigation:

    (b) flooding:

    (c) wildlife:

    (d) foreign opinion:

On balance, do you think the scheme is a good idea? Write arguments for and against the Three Gorges Scheme, then hold a class debate to discuss the issues.

Case Study: **Indian Ocean Tsunami Disaster**

On Boxing Day (26 December) 2004 an earthquake occurred beneath the Indian Ocean off the coast of Sumatra. The resulting tsunami caused the biggest natural disaster in modern times, leaving over 281,000 people dead (the true figure will never be known) and over a million people homeless.

Causes

Tsunami is a Japanese word meaning 'harbour wave', and is the correct name for a wave caused by an earthquake. (It is not a 'tidal' wave.) When an earthquake occurs at a meeting of two **tectonic plates**, massive amounts of energy are released. If the **epicentre** is beneath the ocean an enormous volume of water can be displaced. This creates a ripple effect - just like when a bowl of jelly is disturbed. Tsunamis can also be caused by land slides and volcanic eruptions.

Effects

Despite a four-hour delay between the earthquake that registered 8.9 on the Richter scale, and the waves reaching the shore, no warning was given. No warning system exists in the Indian Ocean like that in the Pacific, based in Hawaii. It was at the peak of the holiday season, and places such as Phuket in Thailand were packed with foreign tourists, sun bathing, swimming, diving, or relaxing in their hotel rooms. So no-one was prepared for the series of devastating waves which struck the coastline around the Indian Ocean, affecting eleven countries, including Sri Lanka, India, Bangladesh, Thailand, Malaysia and Indonesia, as well as the Maldives, Andaman and Nicobar islands, not to mention thousands of small, isolated islets. In low-lying regions the waves reached two kilometres inland. Some islands were so low, there was no-where to run to. In some places whole villages were completely swept away.

The Development of the Tsunami

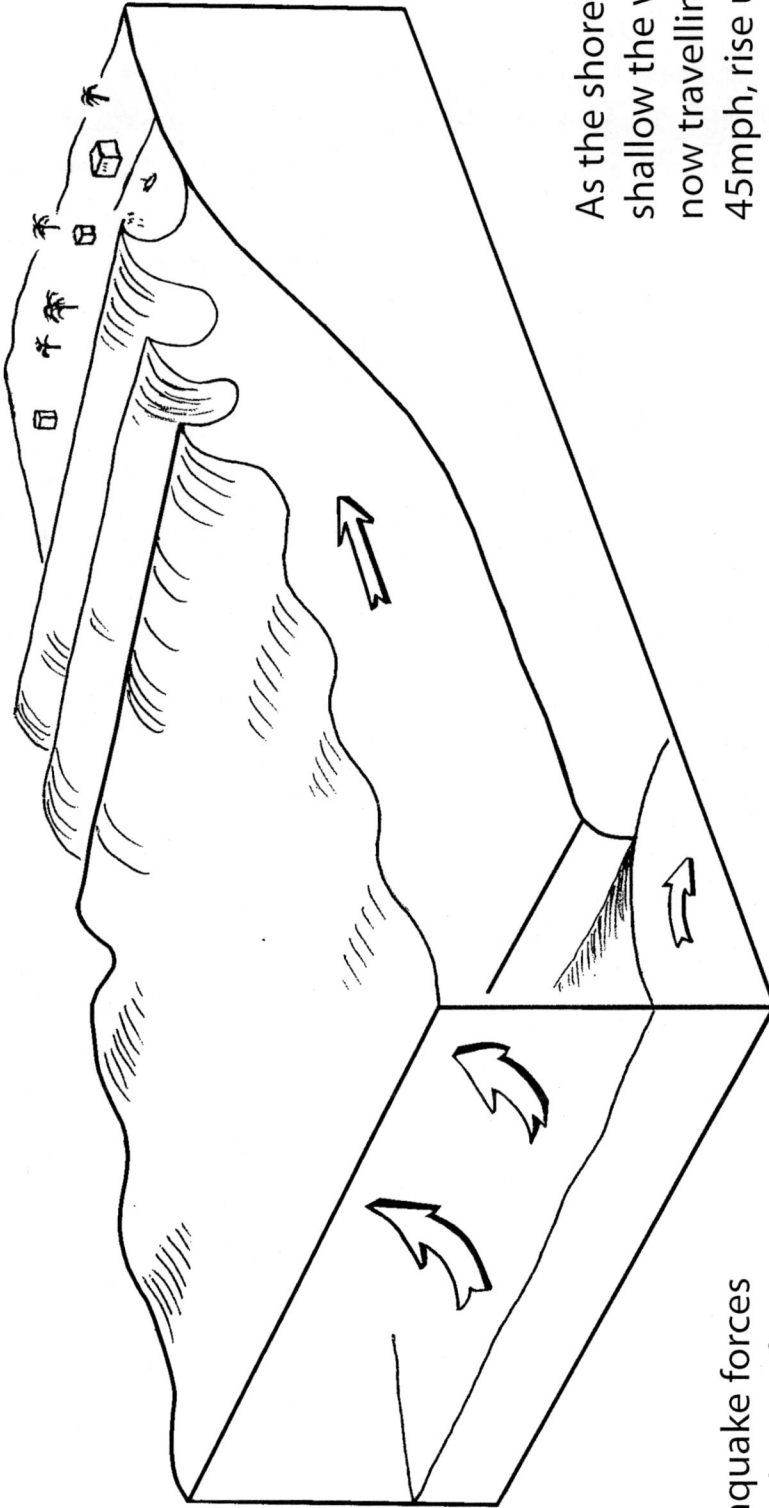

As the shore gets shallow the waves, now travelling at 45mph, rise upwards.

In deep water the tsunami travels at speeds of up to 500mph.

An earthquake forces a huge volume of water to be displaced.

The Aftermath

After the initial shock, the first task was to look for survivors, particularly lost family members. People had been swept out to sea, others buried under debris or trapped in their hotel rooms. Sadly, the death toll gradually increased, and the number of people missing was even greater. Over a million people were left with no fresh water, food, or medical supplies. Soon an international aid effort was launched - the largest to date, costing over a billion pounds. As no clean water supplies remained and there was inadequate sanitation, some five million people were at risk from water-borne diseases such as cholera. In Sri Lanka relief operations were also hampered by monsoon rains and flash floods that left roads and bridges impassable, even for large lorries carrying relief supplies.

1)   **Find the Indian Ocean in an atlas.**

    (a) **Either write down the names of countries and islands that were affected,**

or   (b) **Using a blank map of the Indian Ocean, try to locate the epicentre of the earthquake off the coast of Sumatra, then use a compass to draw concentric rings radiating out from it. Now plot the countries that would have been affected.**

2)   **What could have been done to reduce the death toll?**

3)   **How could a relief operation be organised for such a disaster? Try to think of the short-term and long term needs of the survivors.**

4)   **What could be done to avoid a similar tragedy in the future?**

Chapter Nine

Water on Maps

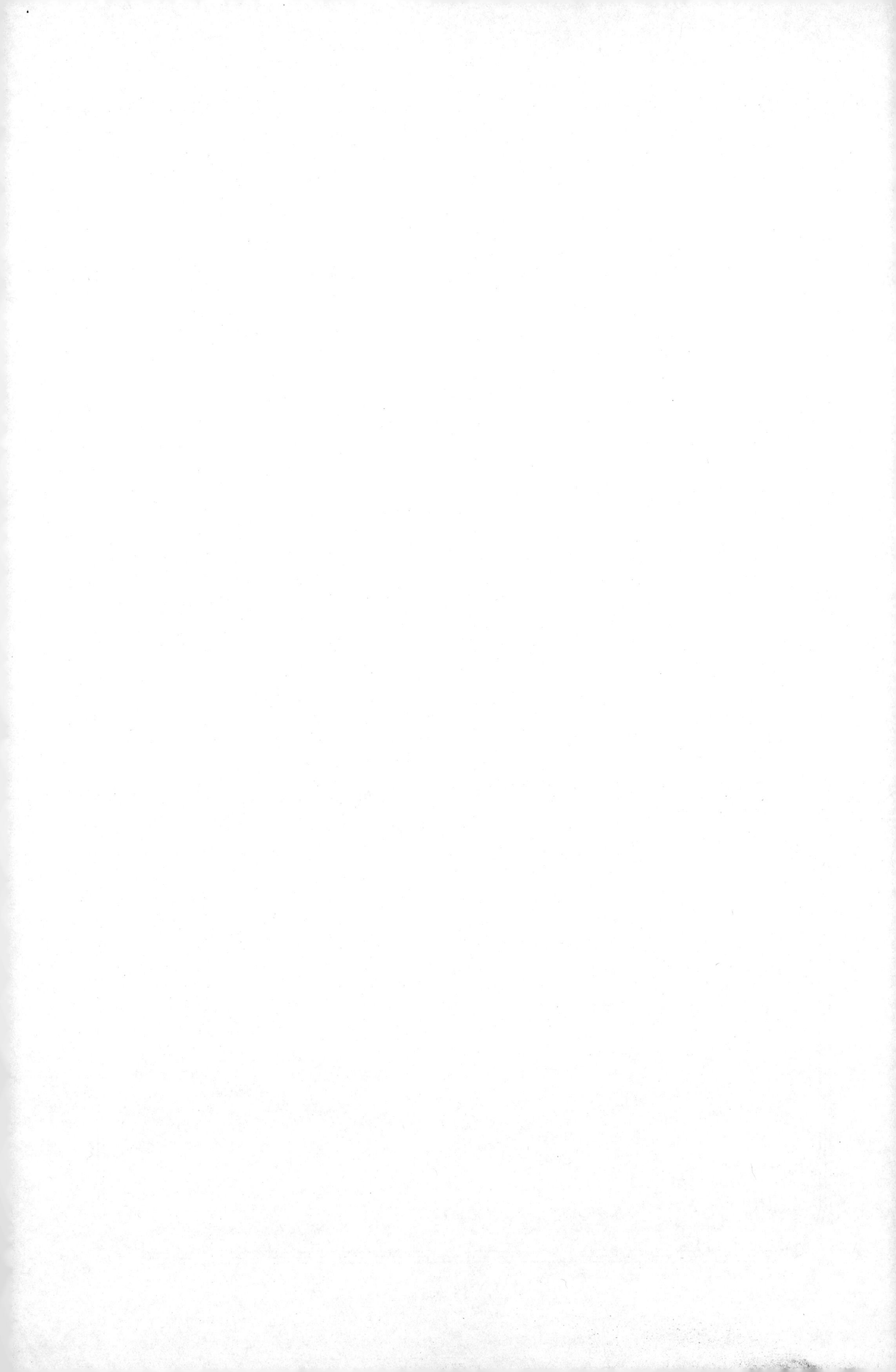

Water on Maps

Finding Water Features

On Ordnance Survey maps water features are represented as light blue symbols. However, care must be taken not to confuse these with tourist information which is also represented as a darker blue. Places can be identified on a map using the grid references marked on either side or at the top or bottom of the map. These are given as four or six-figure references. Always give the horizontal numbers before the vertical ones, and if in doubt remember the phrase 'along the passage, then up the stairs'.

Directions

The top of the map always faces north, unless it is stated otherwise.

Finding the Direction of Flow

Fact: rivers always flow downhill. So to find the direction in which the river is flowing first of all look for any spot heights near the river. The highest numbers will be nearest the source. If no spot heights are present then look at the nearest contour lines, identify their heights, and work it out from those.

Unless the pattern of contour lines is very complex, they will also reveal the shape of the valley, as they form a U-shaped pattern with the bottom of the U (the highest land) towards the source.

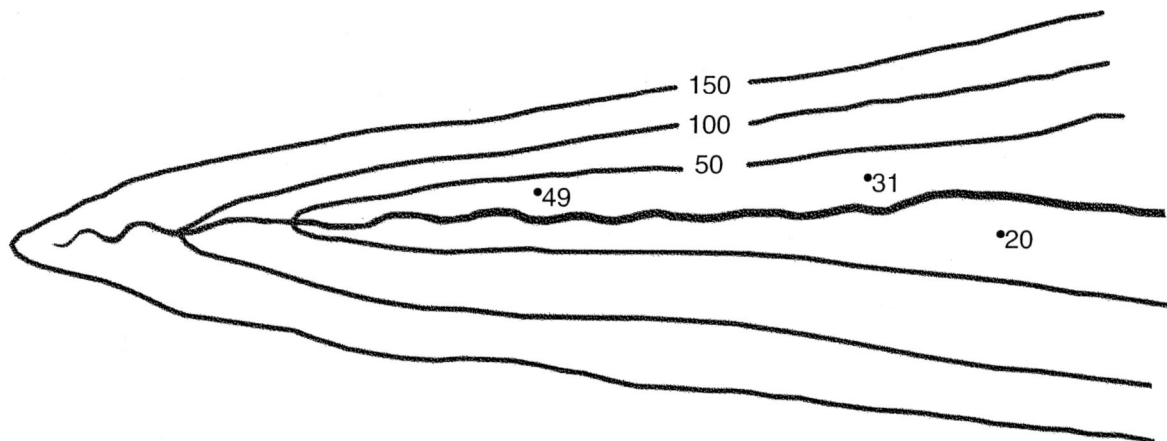

1) **In which direction is the river flowing?**

Measuring Distances

The correct way to measure distances on a map is to use a length of scrap paper. Placing the corner of the paper on the starting point, lay the paper along the map, then mark the destination with a pencil. The distance along the paper can then be measured against the grid squares, as each square, regardless of the scale of an OS map, equals one kilometre square.

Sadly, river features are rarely straight, and the technique is slightly more complicated when measuring curved lines. Still use a piece of paper, as string will stretch, and use the same technique, but follow the feature by revolving the edge of the paper around the pencil point. Then mark the final length with a pencil mark and measure it against the scale.

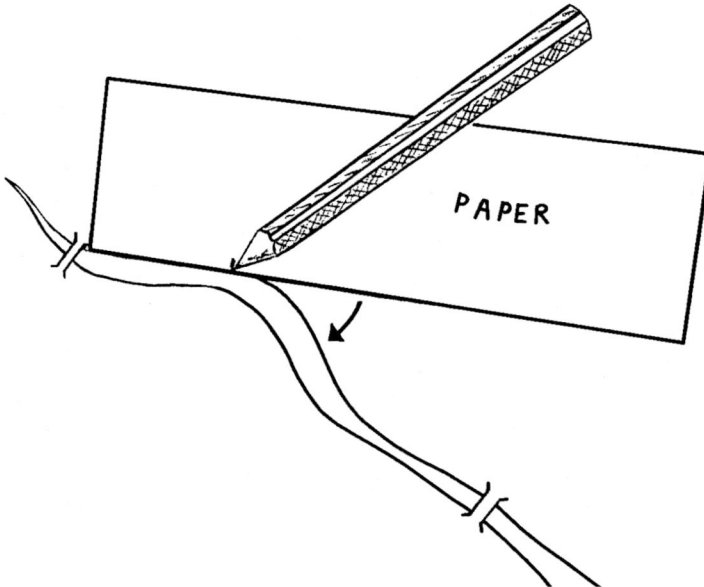

PAPER

Measuring Areas

A common question in examinations is to find the area of a feature such as a reservoir, lake or wood. The easiest way to do this is to:

a)   **Add up all the complete grid squares that are seen inside the feature. Remember, each square on the map represents one km^2**

b) Try to match different part-squares, so that they appear to make complete squares. Then add these to your total, along with any remaining fractions. Remember, your answer will be in kilometres square (km^2)

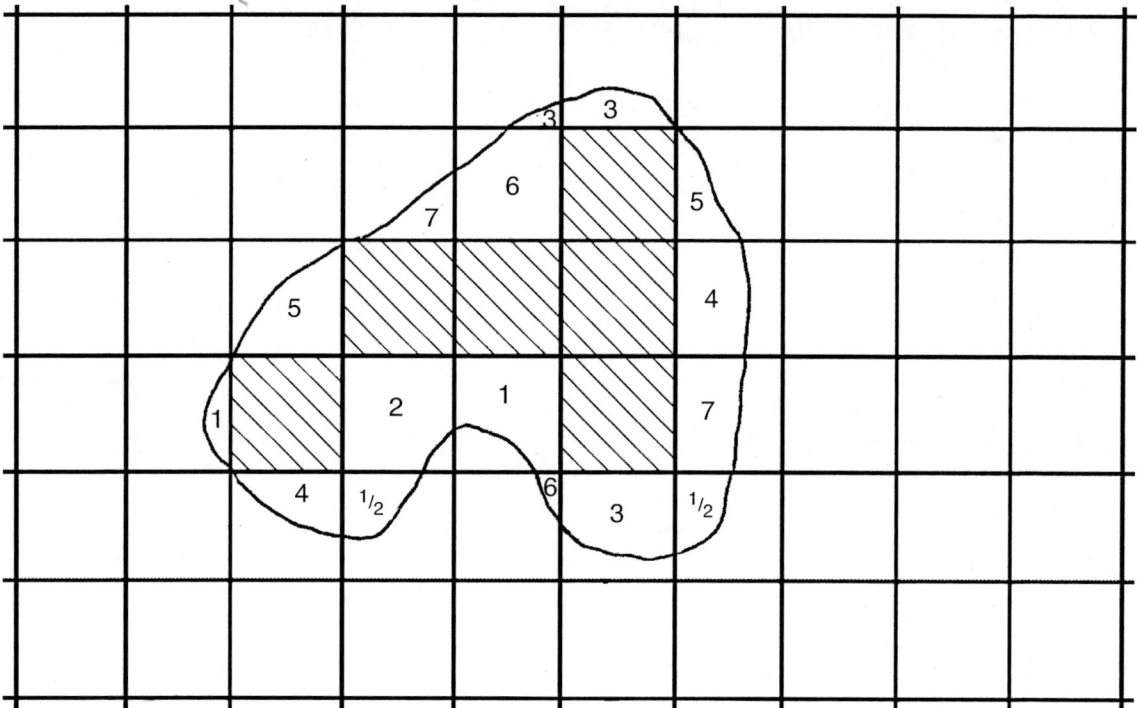

S **2) What is the area of the shape shown in the diagram above?**

Drawing Cross Sections

A good way of determining the shape of the land is to draw a cross section. This is a diagram which shows what the landscape would look like if it was cut through with a knife (or bulldozer!). In other words, what you see is similar to a loaf of bread that has been sliced.

Look at the diagram on the next page. It shows the contour lines from a map, bisected by a section line (A to B). Beneath them horizontal lines have been drawn to show the height, as represented by the contours (O metres (sea level) to 200 metres). To draw a cross section, place a ruler vertically across the two diagrams. Then, as you carefully move the ruler from left to right, plot a cross on the horizontal line that represents the height of a particular contour every time the ruler meets the section line where it goes over a contour line. When you have reached the end draw a free-hand line to join up the crosses.

3) Try to complete the cross section below.

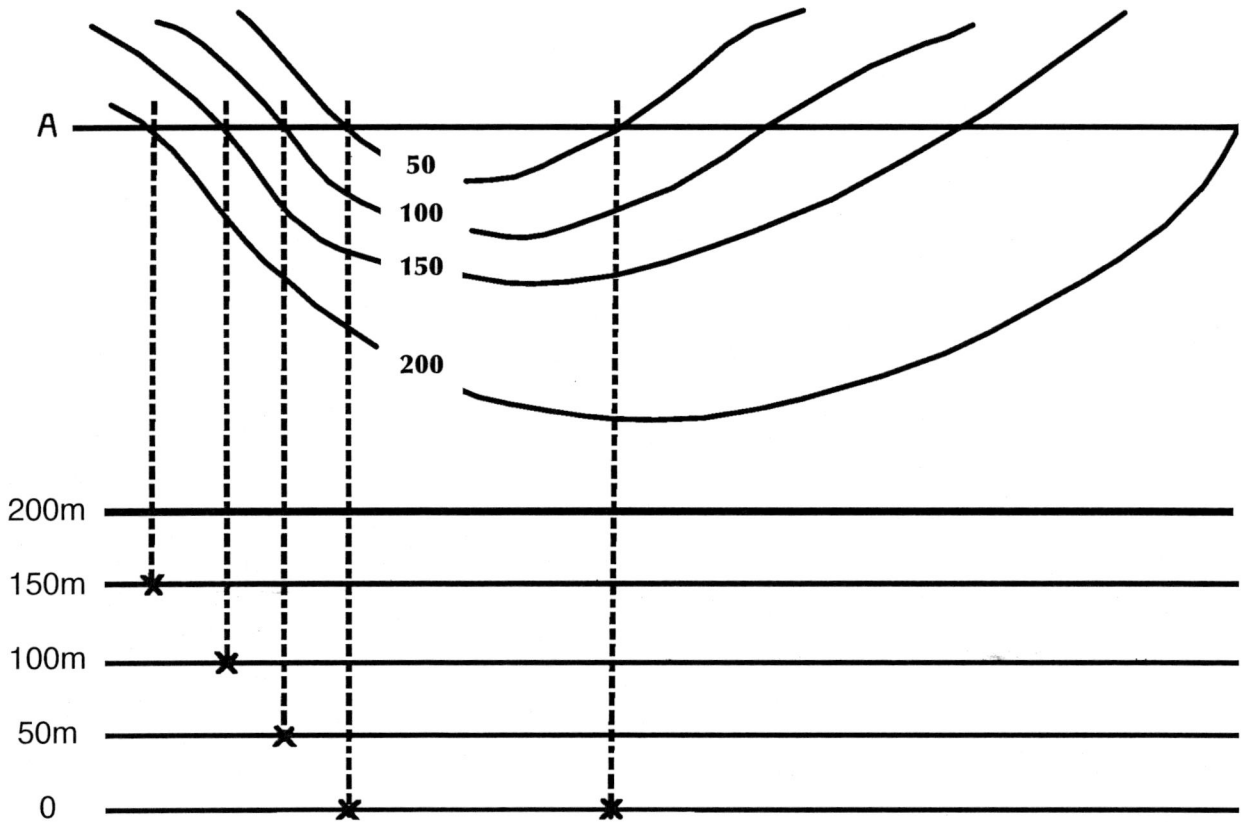

Transects

A transect is simply a cross section with labels added to identify significant physical and human features.

4) On black and white sketch maps contour lines are often shown as dashes (See also Figure 7, Chapter 1). Look at the maps and diagrams on the next page. On the left are pictures, on the right are maps. Your task is to try to draw a map of what is shown in the picture, or a picture of what the map is representing. Try to use the correct map symbols and colours. To help you, the features have been listed on the right-hand side. *Tip:* If you are successful the river should flow continuously from the top of the page to the bottom.

Picture	Map	Features
		Spring Valley Tributary Confluence Windmill Ruin
		Road Bridge Car Park Mill Electricity Transmission lines
		Church Windpump Coniferous Wood Roads Bridge Lake Telephone Box Golf Course Braiding Campsite
		Radio Mast Tumulus Passenger Ferry Salting Slopes Lighthouse Beacon Groynes Pier

Fieldwork

An examination of a river or stream can make an interesting and worthwhile topic for fieldwork. This could be based on **physical** or **human** elements. For example, as **physical geography** one could look at various river features that may be found along a given stretch of river. These could then be compared with those that would be found in a major river system. A river survey could be linked to a study of the weather over a period of time, perhaps comparing the depth of water at a ford with the amount of rainfall at a given time. A more advanced study might examine whether there is any delay between a period of heavy rainfall and a rise in the river's depth.

A study in **human geography** may focus on man's use of a particular river, be it for transport, industry, or leisure activities. A study could also be made of water treatment, either for the provision of fresh drinking water or sewage treatment (see Chapter 3).

Answers

Chapter One

Page 11 - *Case Study:* The Grand Canyon

The Grand Canyon in the USA has been created by the ***Colorado*** River. In places it is over 1,900 metres deep and 24 km. wide. It was formed as the powerful river cut rapidly downwards - a process known as ***vertical*** erosion - leaving the ***rock strata*** exposed. ***Lateral*** or sideways erosion was far less pronounced, relying on weathering. Rain cut grooves in the valley sides (**physical** weathering), crystals growing in cracks crumbled the rock (**chemical** weathering), while tree roots and burrowing animals (**biological** weathering) also helped to break up the rock. This has left blocks of ***loosened rock***, and unstable ***scree slopes*** of loose stones, while in places harder rock that was not eroded so easily juts out forming ***overhangs***.

Page 12 - (a) ***Arizona*** (b) ***Lake Mead*** (c) ***Hoover Dam*** (d) ***Las Vegas***

Page 13 - 1) **The load of a river will depend on the volume of water, the speed of the current and the nature of the geology through which the river flows.**

2) **The greater the discharge, or volume of water in a river, the greater its capacity to carry the load.**

3) & 4) See separate map, page 104

Page 14 - *Case Study:* The Somerset Levels

2) See separate map, page 105

3) **The general trend of the rivers is SE to NW.**

4) **The Duke of Monmouth's forces were routed on 6 July 1685. They lost their element of surprise when one of the rebels stumbled into a rhyne and his musket discharged, alerting the king's forces. Monmouth was captured and executed nine days later.**

5) **Place-name evidence includes Bridgewater, Axbridge, Wells and Nailsea.**

6) **The low-lying area around Glastonbury Tor would once have been submerged.**

Page 16 - 8) **There are many different interest groups, so a balance has to be struck between them, whilst preserving this important wetland environment.**

Page 18 - *Extension Work* - World River Features

Some guidance may be useful in the use of an atlas. It is suggested that the children find the answers using the relevant maps, then check their answers using the index.

1) **Source - Lake Victoria (White Nile).**

2) **Waterfall - Angel Falls, Venezuela.**

3) **Rapids - Cedar Rapids, USA.**

4) **Gorge - Grand Canyon, USA.**

5) **Confluence - The White Nile and Blue Nile at Khartoum, Sudan.**

6) **Meanders - The Seine at Rouen, France.**

7) **Flood Plain - Mississippi, USA.**

8) **Bluffs - Pine Bluff on the Arkansas River, USA.**

9) **Delta - Nile, Egypt.**

10) **Estuary - Thames, UK.**

Chapter Two

2) **Make sure taps are turned off; don't use more water than is necessary; shower rather than bath; collect rainwater for watering plants.**

3) **People in L.E.D.Cs are more likely to be careful with water because they might well have limited and irregular supplies, and may have to carry it long distances.**

2) **Most of these countries have hot climates and are L.E.D.Cs.**

3) **The Aral Sea has experienced a dramatic drop in water level in recent years, particularly because of the need to irrigate cotton fields by diverting rivers that would otherwise flow into the Aral Sea. There has been a catastrophic increase in salinity and pollution, contributing to a range of serious health problems for people living in the region.**

4) **Britain faces an ever-growing demand for water, supplies are finite, and are often not in the most populated regions.**

5) **Similar geographical problems affect many L.E.D.Cs.**

6) **A 'national grid` of water supplies could alleviate the problems.**

1			R	U	T	L	A	N	D	**WATER**
2		K	I	E	L	D	E	R		**WATER**
3		S	E	L	S	E	T			
4	C	O	W	G	R	E	E	N		
5				G	R	A	F	H	A	M	**WATER**
6	E	L	A	N	V	A	L	L	E	Y
7			R	O	A	D	F	O	R	D
8	H	A	N	N	I	N	G	F	I	E	L	D
9		D	E	R	W	E	N	T
10	C	A	R	S	I	N	G	T	O	N

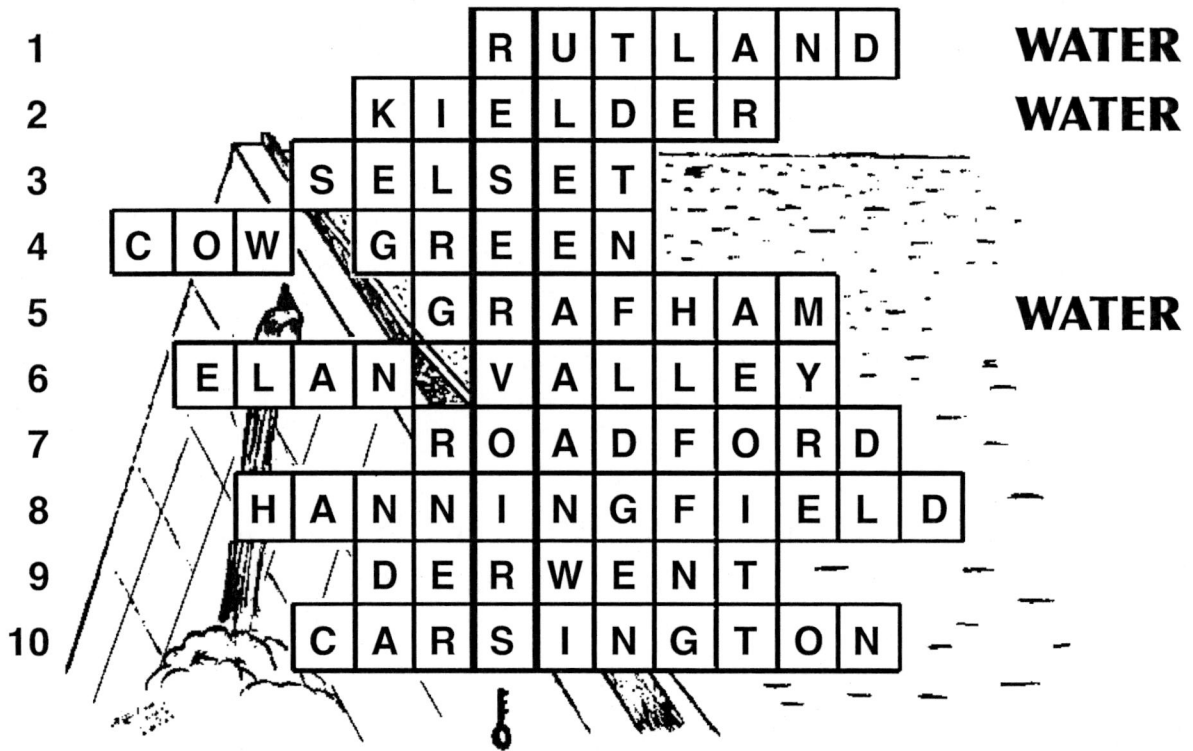

Page 29 - *Inputs and Outputs*

Inputs: (a) **Hail**   (d) **Rainwater from a roof**   (i) **Sleet**   (j) **Rainfall**
(g) **Snowmelt on a mountainside**

Outputs: (b) **Waste water from a sink**   (c) **Sprinklers**   (e) **Sewage outfall**
(f) **A car wash**   (h) **Waste water from a washing machine**

94

Chapter Three

Page 36 - 1) See separate sheet, page 106.

2) **There has been much debate about the merits of chlorination. It does improve dental health, however it has been suggested that too much chlorine in drinking water could actually lead to a number of health problems.**

Page 39 - 4) Some advantages and disadvantages of tap water and bottled water include:

Tap water: Cheap and readily available, however it is all treated in a uniform manner, including the addition of chlorine.

Bottled: A wide variety of choice, and with differing mineral contents, however it is relatively expensive and some of dubious benefit.

5) **There is an argument for not treating all water to the same standard, but this would require a complicated and expensive duplication of water mains.**

Chapter Four

Page 43 - *The Impacts of Flooding*

Negative Aspects: **buildings - foundations**

                               Farms - crops; animals

                               Economic - pay

                               Transport - roads; railway.

                               Water Supplies - contaminated; diseases

                               People - accommodation

Page 48 - *Flood Simulation*

        3)   (a) See map on page 104

                (b) Some roads and houses would be flooded.

Chapter Five

Page 55 - 1) (a) **26° N**   (b) **50$^1/_2$°E**   (e) **Persian Gulf**   (f) **Saudi Arabia**
(g) **Desert and semi-desert**

Page 56 - 2) **Desalination is the process whereby salt water is turned into fresh water.**

3) **The Al Hidd Desalination Plant cost $360 million.**

4) **The water table has dropped and the ground water supply could have run out if no action was taken.**

5) **30 million gallons of fresh water a day can now be produced.**

6) **Storage tanks, pipelines and pumps were also required to distribute and water.**

Clearly the practical science exercise to produce fresh water will require the right equipment and constant supervision.

(a) **A large amount of heat (energy) is required to extract fresh water, as the water has to be boiled off and the fresh water condensed.**

(b) **Salt is a by-product that can be a valuable additional resource.**

Chapter Six

Page 59

1) **Pollution is often caused by man's careless disposal of waste materials into rivers, lakes and the sea. (This ranges from easily biodegradable material to nuclear waste that will remain with us for thousands of years).**

2) **In 2005 some 10,000 children die every day from cholera and other water related diseases.**

3) **The safest place to extract water in mountainous areas is as close to the source as possible, i.e. before it can become polluted.**

4) **(Using encyclopedias, the internet, etc).**

Page 60 5) **In Britain water pollution may be caused by industry, farms (including the leaching of chemicals and farm slurry) as well as domestic waste. Unforeseen accidents may also occur, such as oil spills.**

6) **The easiest one to deal with is probably our own domestic waste. It only takes a little thought about how we throw things away, be it a crisp packet, an old bottle or waste engine oil from a car or cooking oil from a fat fryer.**

7) **Pollution does matter, for in the end it affects us all, as well as future generations.**

8) **Ecosystem (see Glossary, page 111).**

Page 62 - *The Shetlands Oil Disaster*

1) **The capital of the Shetland Isles is Lerwick.**

2) **The tanker *Braer* was carrying 85,000 tonnes of light crude oil, as well as 500 tonnes of fuel oil to run the ship's engines.**

3) **The oil slick spread quickly because of the Sumburgh Roost tidal race, as well as the tides carrying it into the shore, and currents moving it along the coast.**

4) **The oil affected the food chain, for larger creatures such as seals depend on the affected fish.**

5) (a) **Sea birds in danger include the great northern diver, black guillemot, eider duck, long-tailed duck and sea cormorant.**

6) *Braer* **went aground in the Shetlands because the islands lie in the shipping lanes between Norway and its destination, Canada.**

7) **Liberia is in west Africa.**

Chapter Seven

Page 71

For tidal turbines:

Non-polluting; cheap, once installed; reduces the need for fossil fuels and nuclear power; the technology could be sold abroad; less contentious than wind farms.

Against:

Still at the experimental stage; a danger to shipping; visual impact; transferring the power to the shore; limited number of potential sites; initial costs.

Chapter Eight

Page 77 - *Three Gorges Fact File*

1) **Latitude: 31° N**
2) **Longitude: 110° E**
3) **Number of dams: one**
4) **The cost: 25-32 billion US dollars**
5) **Number of people re-housed: 1.2 - 1.9 million people**
6) **Number of cities submerged: 13**
7) **Number of towns submerged: 140**
8) **Number of villages submerged: 1,352**
9) **Area to be submerged: 1,000 km^2**
10) **Amount of rock moved: over 100 million tonnes**
11) **The amount of power to be produced: 17,680 - 18.2 million kilowatts**
12) **The effect on:**
    (a) **navigation: This should be easier. A ship-lock will allow passage past the dam.**
    (b) **flooding: The dam and reservoir will control flooding on the Yangtze, which has caused the deaths of over 300,000 people since 1900.**
    (c) **wildlife: Yangtze river dolphins, Siberian cranes and Chinese alligators will lose their natural habitats and could face extinction.**
    (d) **foreign opinion: This has been mixed. Some countries see it as a brave move towards modernisation, others as a potential environmental disaster.**

Page 80 - *Indian Ocean Tsunami Disaster*

1) (a) **The countries and islands affected included Sri Lanka, India, Bangladesh, Myanmar (Burma), Thailand, Malaysia, Indonesia; even Somalia in east Africa, as well as small island groups including the Maldives, Andaman and Nicobar islands.**

   (b) See enclosed map, 107

2) **An early warning system, like the one operated in the Pacific.**

3) **Relief operations:**

Short term **help needs to provide fresh drinking water, food and shelter, whilst efforts need to be made to re-unite families and help locate missing people.**

In the *long term*, the infrastructure needs to be re-built, and large amounts of money need to be found.

Perhaps a dedicated international agency should be established, which could be on call to deal with any future disasters.

4) **An early warning system could prevent a similar disaster.**

Chapter Nine

Page 83 - 1) West to east.

2) Six whole squares + $7^1/_2$ part-squares = $13^1/_2$ km^2

Page 87 - See separate sheet, page 108.

Chapter 1
The Flood Plain

Key

- Watershed
- Springs
- River Cliff
- Slope
- Low Lying (50m or less)
- High Land (150m or above)

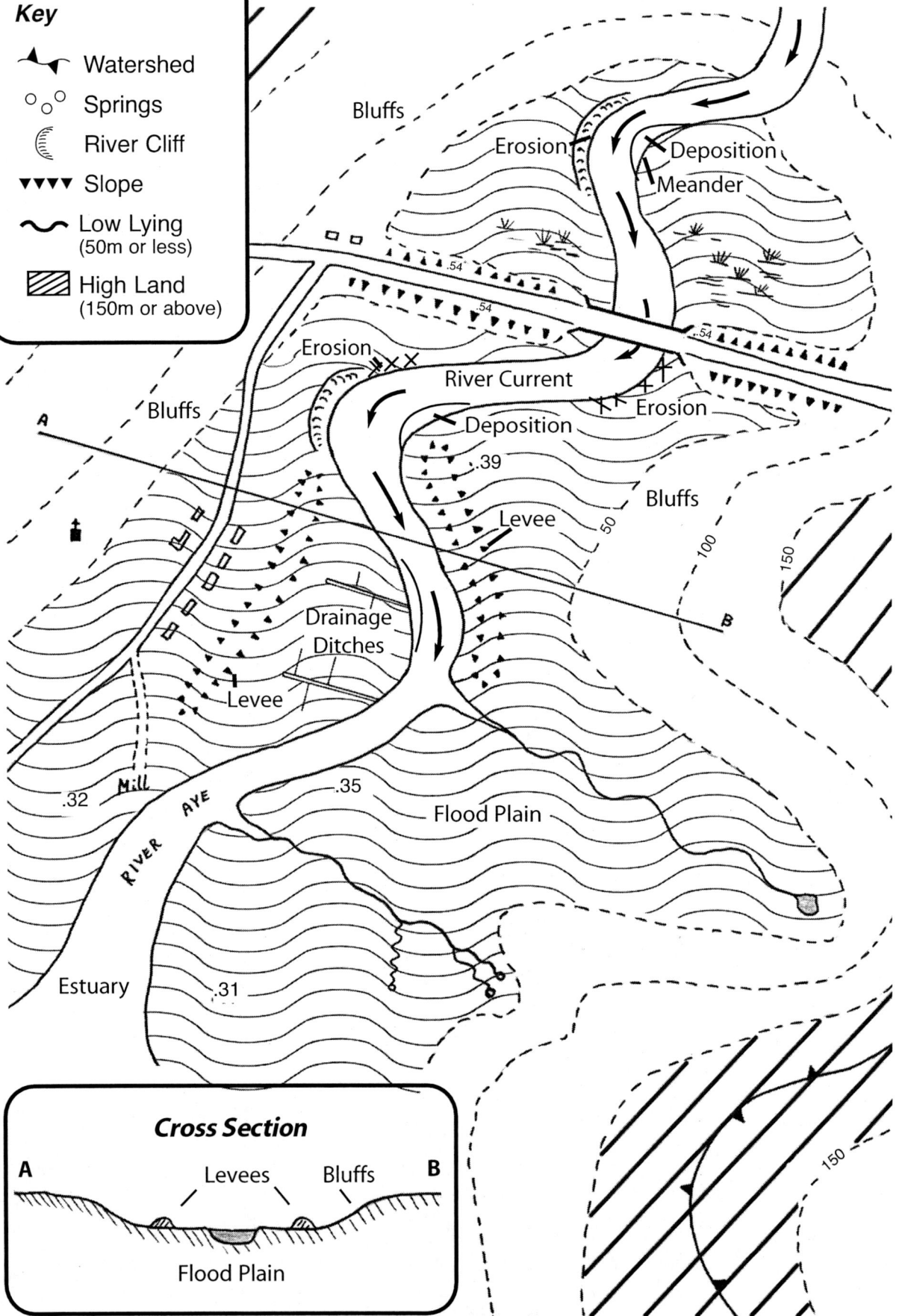

Bluffs

Erosion

Deposition

Meander

.54

.54

.54

Erosion

River Current

Deposition

Erosion

Bluffs

Bluffs

.39

.50

100

150

Levee

A

B

Drainage Ditches

Levee

.32 Mill

RIVER AYE

.35

Flood Plain

Estuary

.31

150

Cross Section

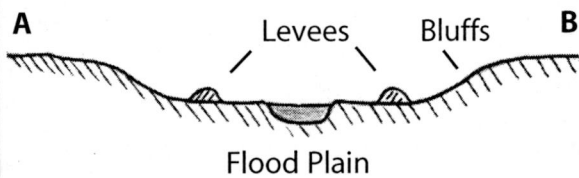

A

Levees

Bluffs

B

Flood Plain

Case Study: The Somerset Levels

Figure 5

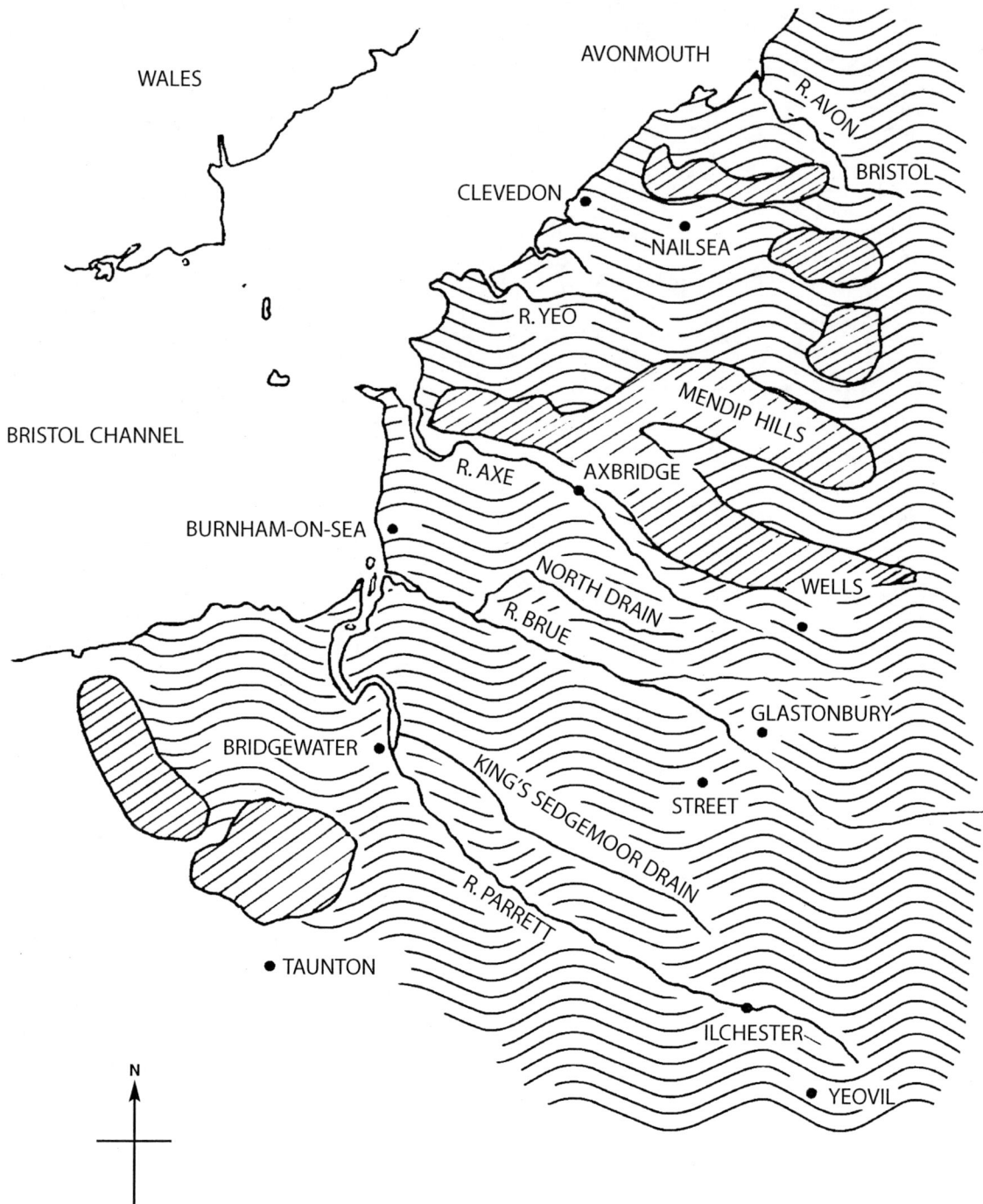

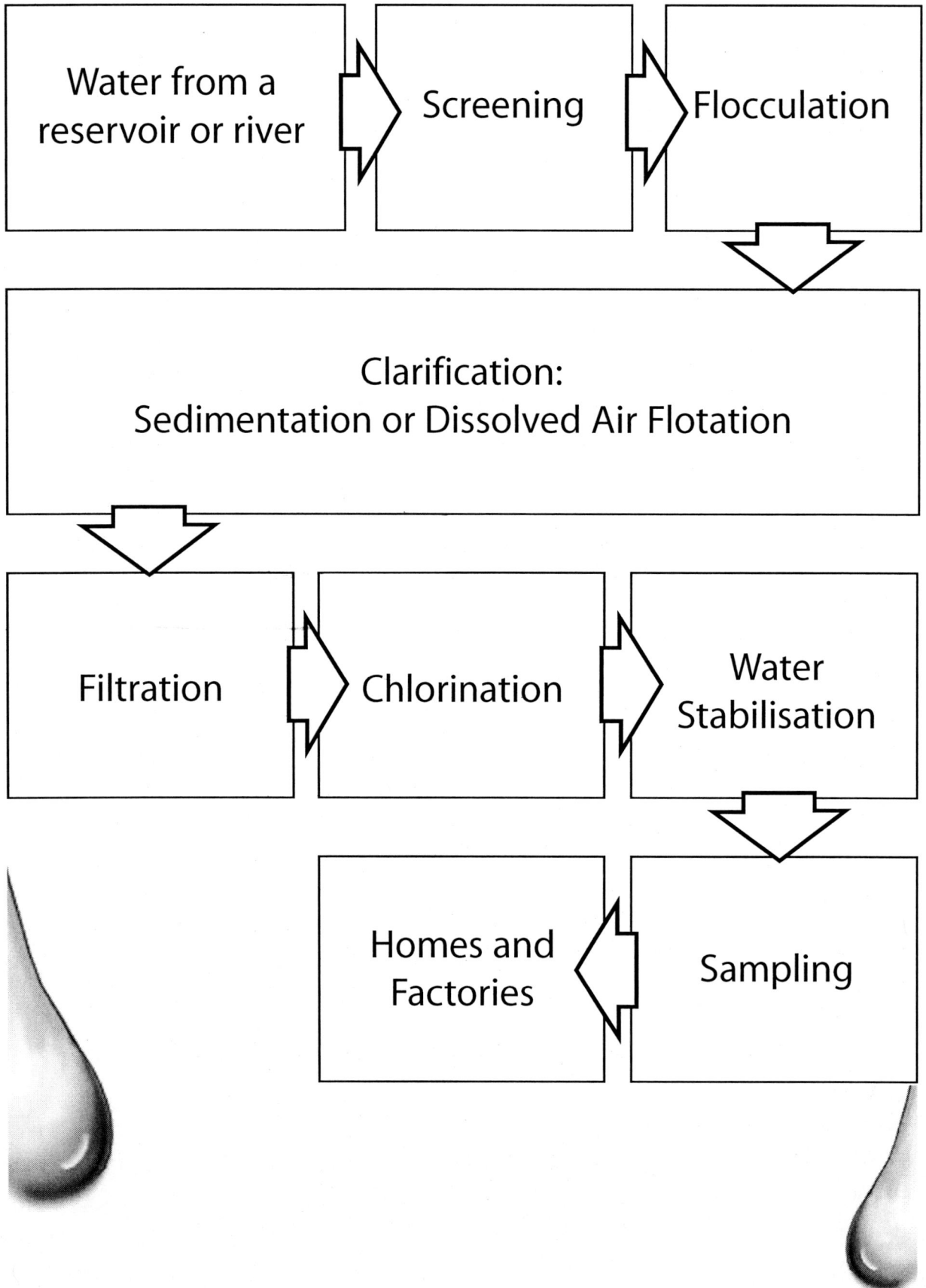

```
┌─────────────────────┐    ┌─────────────────┐    ┌─────────────────┐
│   Water from a      │ ⇒  │    Screening    │ ⇒  │   Flocculation  │
│  reservoir or river │    │                 │    │                 │
└─────────────────────┘    └─────────────────┘    └─────────────────┘
                                                            ⇓
┌──────────────────────────────────────────────────────────────────┐
│                         Clarification:                             │
│          Sedimentation or Dissolved Air Flotation                  │
└──────────────────────────────────────────────────────────────────┘
          ⇓
┌─────────────────┐    ┌─────────────────┐    ┌─────────────────┐
│   Filtration    │ ⇒  │   Chlorination  │ ⇒  │      Water      │
│                 │    │                 │    │  Stabilisation  │
└─────────────────┘    └─────────────────┘    └─────────────────┘
                                                        ⇓
                       ┌─────────────────┐    ┌─────────────────┐
                       │   Homes and     │ ⇐  │    Sampling     │
                       │   Factories     │    │                 │
                       └─────────────────┘    └─────────────────┘
```

Chapter 8

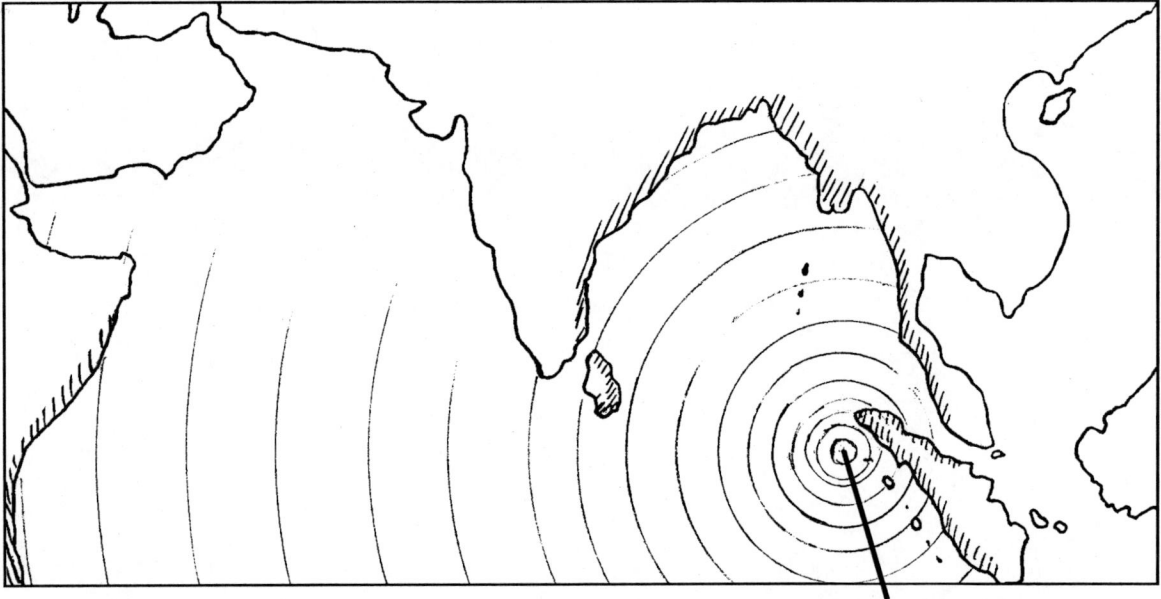

Affected Areas

Epicentre of 8.9 magnitude
quake off the coast of Sumatra.

Picture	Map	Features
		Spring Valley Tributary Confluence Windmill Ruin
		Road Bridge Car Park Mill Electricity Transmission lines
		Church Windpump Coniferous Wood Roads Bridge Lake Telephone Box Golf Course Braiding Campsite
		Radio Mast Tumulus Passenger Ferry Salting Slopes Lighthouse Beacon Groynes Pier

Glossary

Water Glossary

General

Desalination - turning salt water (saline water or brine) into fresh water.

Desertification - the change from an area being fertile to one with arid, desert conditions, often caused by human interference.

Ecosystem - a community of plants and animals that are dependent upon the interaction of all the elements that make it up.

Epicentre - the point of maximum impact of an earthquake on the earth's surface.

Erosion - the wearing away of rock.

Geology - the study ot the earth and rocks.

Global Warming - rising global temperatures, possibly caused by pollution.

Impermeable - does not allow water to pass through.

Irrigation - providing water for crops.

Knoll - an isolated hill.

L.E.D.C - Less Economically Developed Country.

M.E.D.C - More Economically Developed Country.

Permeable - allows water to pass through, like a sponge, or to penetrate along joints.

Pollution - harmful or undesirable substances damaging the environment.

Porous - allows water to pass through (see permeable).

Ridge - land rising to a pronounced peak.

Saturated - the soil is unable to absorb any more rain water.

Tectonic plates - large sections or 'plates' which together form the earth's crust.

Tsunami - a large wave caused by an earthquake, landslide or meteorite.

Velocity - speed in a straight line. e.g. water falling from a waterfall.

Water Harvesting - collecting rain water so that it may be used for domestic purposes.

Weathering - the natural breakdown of rocks by rainwater, the sun, chemicals, plants or animals.

Rivers

Aquifer - water trapped below ground in porous rock.

Attrition - erosion caused by colliding stones.

Bluff - fairly steep banks formed from former spurs.

Bore hole - a hole drilled in the ground in order to reach a water supply, such as an aquifer.

Braiding - Where the river splits up, then re-joins later.

Catchment Area - the area from which a river collects its water.

Condensation - water produced when water vapour cools, e.g. against a window.

Confluence - where two rivers meet.

Corrosion - some rocks, like limestone, dissolve in water.

Delta - a flat fan of alluvium at the end of some rivers, e.g. the Mississippi Delta.

Dendritic - tree-like, such as drainage patterns that mirror the shape of a tree.

Deposition - the dropping of eroded material.

Discharge - the amount of water in a river, measured in cubic metres per second.

Drainage basin - the area from which the river collects its water.

Drainage ditch - a ditch used to drain marshy low-lying land.

Dyke - embankments built to protect an area from flooding.

Eddies - swirling water created by an obstruction.

Estuary - the wide mouth of a river, formed from a flooded valley.

Evaporation - to change from a liquid to a gas, e.g. water into water vapour.

Flash flood - a sudden flood, often caused by heavy, localised rainfall.

Flood plain - the flat plain which a river crosses in the old age stage.

Flood relief channels - ditches dug to carry away excess water.

Gorge (or canyon) - a steep-sided valley created by powerful vertical erosion.

Hydraulic Action - like the action of waves against cliffs, the river traps air in cracks and hollows and wears away the river channel.

Hydrological cycle - the perpetual movement of water, from evaporation to precipitation etc.

Interception - raindrops prevented from hitting the ground by leaves, roads, buildings etc. (They are intercepted.)

Levees - natural or man-made banks at the sides of rivers to contain flood water.

Load - the amount of silt and sediment carried by a river.

Meander - twisting, as when the river snakes.

Percolation - rain water soaking into the ground.

Plunge Pool - the deep pool formed at the foot of a waterfall.

Rapids - small waterfalls.

Regime - the seasonal variation of volume in a river.

River system - the complete river and its tributaries, from the source to the sea.

Sediment or alluvium - eroded material, transported and deposited by a river.

Silt - deposits of mud, sand, clay etc. (alluvium)

Source - the start of a river.

Spate - the river in full-flow, when flooding is most likely to occur.

Spur - an area of land projecting into a river valley.

Traction - rolling and tumbling of rocks along a river bed, particularly during a flood.

Transportation - the river's ability to carry loose materials.

Watershed - the divide between two catchment areas or drainage basins.

Water table - the level of water trapped beneath the ground.

Wetland - an area of low-lying land that is permanently or occasionally flooded.

Water Treatment

Aeration - mixing air with water, increasing oxygen levels and lowering quantities of carbon dioxide.

Chlorination - adding chlorine to water.

Coagulation - a process used to remove fine particles.

Filtration - filtering to remove unwanted particles and algae.

Reservoir - a store of water.

Softening - reducing the levels of dissolved calcium and magnesium.

Cross-curricular Links

Cross-curricular Links

Art

1)   Try to find copies of some of the following works of art:

Snowstorm - Steamboat off a Harbour's Mouth (1842) J. M. W. Turner
The Bathers, Asnières (1883-4) George Seurat
The Lady of Shalott (1888) John William Waterhouse
The Gulf Stream (1899) Winslow Homer
Waterlilies (c. 1920) Claude Monet
The Splash or A Bigger Splash (1960s) David Hockney
Cataract 3 (1967) Bridget Riley

Look at the different ways in which water has been depicted. Which do you think works best and why?

Have a go at creating your own drawing or painting to depict a mood, such as a still lake, reflections on the surface of a dark pond, or a stormy sea.

Try to find out about the story behind one of the paintings.

2) Reflections

You will need: old magazines or travel brochures, paper and glue.

(a) Create a collage by tearing watery colours from a magazine, arranging them in a random pattern and sticking them on to a piece of paper.

(b) You may like to add pictures of yachts or other water sports, either drawn by yourself or cut from a magazine or travel brochure.

(c) Coat your picture with a layer of P.V.A. glue to give it a watery sheen.

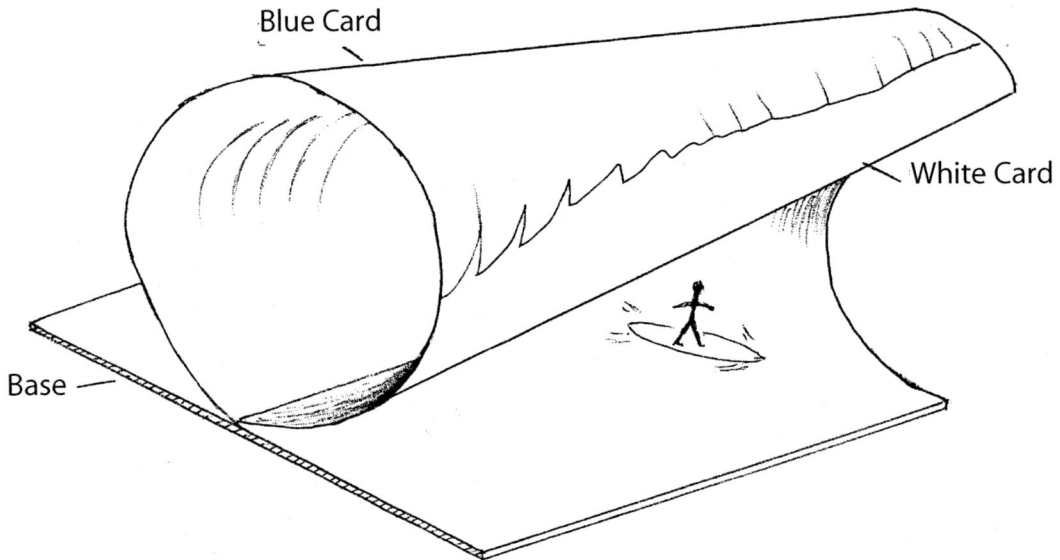

3) **Surf Wave**

You will need: blue and white card, and a piece of stiff card or a board for a base.

Blue Card

White Card

Base

4) **A Waterfall**

You will need: a cardboard box, a variety of green and blue coloured paper, cotton wool, while some stones or pebbles add a finishing touch.

Ask an adult to cut down both corners of one side of the box, then bend the side backwards to form a base. Work on what was the bottom of the box, using the diagram to help you.

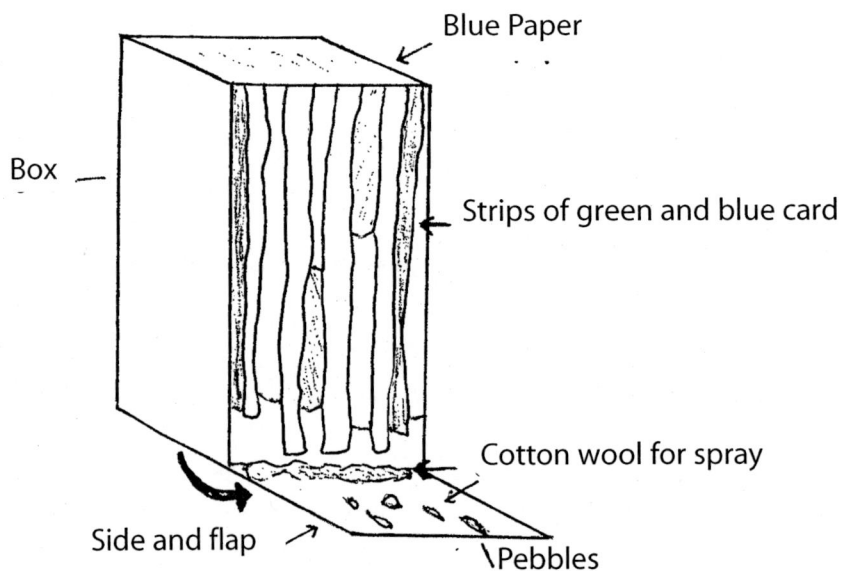

Blue Paper

Box

Strips of green and blue card

Cotton wool for spray

Side and flap

Pebbles

Maths

Volume, discharge and flow rates could be studied as part of a project based on water use or rivers. This could lead to an evaluation of different recording techniques and how the results might be portrayed on graphs and charts.

Science

Water Treatment
Make up a sewage soup of a variety of ingredients, adding to some water such things as soil, leaves, toothpaste, vegetable oil, and tissue paper. Then work out the best way of separating them to clean the water.

English

Rain Myths

St Swithin's Day -	St Swithin died on 2 July 862.
	It is said that if it rains on his feast day we can expect 40 days' rain to follow.
St Paul's Day -	25 January.
	"If St Paul's Day be fair and clear, Then it betides a happy year."
Candlemas Day-	2 February
	"If Candlemas be fair and bright, Winter'll have another flight. But if Candlemas Day be clouds and rain, Winter is gone and will not come again."

We are all familiar with "A red sky at night,
Shepherds' delight..."

(a) Which of these ideas do you think is true?

(b) Why do you think these ideas developed?

(c) Are any of them worth holding on to ?

2) Read *The Ancient Mariner* by Samuel Taylor Coleridge.
How is the conflict between fresh and salt water portrayed?

History

1) Find out how water was used to tackle the Great Fire of London in 1666. How do these methods differ from those of a modern fire brigade?

2) Make a study of the River Nile, considering its importance for sustaining life and allowing a major civilisation to flourish.

RE

During the Kumbh Mela in Nasik, India, sadhus - or Hindu holy men - bathe in the River Godavari. Hundreds of thousands of pilgrims travel to take part in the 'Shahi Snan' - or royal bath - at Nasik. Try to find out more about this important religous festival. How often does it take place? What arrangements have to be made to cope with the arrival of so many people?

Citizenship

Make a study of the River Rhine or Danube, looking at the ways in which several countries through which these rivers flow have to co-operate in order to make use of them.

ICT

Useful Websites

Buxton Natural Mineral Water   www.buxtonwater.co.uk

Save Our Seas Foundation   www.SaveOurSeas.com

South West Lakes Trust   www.swlakestrust

South West Water   www.south-west-water.co.uk

Unicef   www.unicef.org.uk

World Water Problems   www.water.org